# MODERN CUSTOMS

AND

# ANCIENT LAWS

## OF RUSSIA

BEING

THE ILCHESTER LECTURES FOR 1889-90


BY

MAXIME KOVALEVSKY

EX-PROFESSOR OF JURISPRUDENCE IN THE
UNIVERSITY OF MOSCOW



THE LAWBOOK EXCHANGE, LTD.

UNION, NEW JERSEY

2000

ISBN 1-58477-017-1

*Printed in the United States of America*
*On Acid-Free Paper*

**The Lawbook Exchange, Ltd.**
965 Jefferson Avenue
Union, New Jersey 07083-8605

*Please see catalogue at rear of this volume*
*or our website* http://www.lawbookexchange.com
*for a selection of our other reprints.*

**Library of Congress Cataloging-in-Publication Data**

Kovalevskiĭ, M.M. (Maksim Maksimovich), 1851-1916.
Modern customs and ancient laws of Russia / by Maxime Kovalevsky.
p. cm.
Originally published: London David Nutt, 1891.
Includes bibliographical references and index.
ISBN 1-58477-017-1
1. Russia—Social life and customs. 2. Law—Russia—History.
3. Russia—Politics and government. 4. Mir. I. Title.
DK32.K88 1999
947—dc21 99-16487
CIP

# MODERN CUSTOMS

AND

# ANCIENT LAWS

# OF RUSSIA

# MODERN CUSTOMS

AND

# ANCIENT LAWS

## OF RUSSIA

BEING

THE ILCHESTER LECTURES FOR 1889-90

BY

MAXIME KOVALEVSKY

EX-PROFESSOR OF JURISPRUDENCE IN THE
UNIVERSITY OF MOSCOW

LONDON
DAVID NUTT, 270–271 STRAND
1891

To the Memory

OF

SIR HENRY MAINE

# PREFACE.

THE six essays here published contain the outline of lectures delivered at the Taylorian Institution, Oxford. The chief purpose of the lecturer was to show how far the ancient laws of Russia have been preserved by the still living customs of the country people, and to what extent the modern political aspirations of the nation are rooted in its historical past.

I hope that those who make use of this small volume will come to the conclusion that the uncontrolled rule of old custom would, in Russia as elsewhere, be equivalent to the preservation of barbarism and oppression.

On the other hand the English reader may very likely alter his mind as to the supposed discontinuity with the past of the movement whose progressive evolution forms the chief interest of modern Russian history.

I am persuaded that the study of the old Russian folkmotes, and that of the Russian Parliaments of the sixteenth and seventeenth centuries, will impress on him the conviction that the modern Russian "idealogues" deserve as little this nickname as those French Liberals, under Napoleon I., whose generous endeavours created modern France. The so-called Sobors, or old Russian Parliaments, constitute for the Russian Liberals a precedent not less important than the one furnished by the "États Généraux" to the school of Benjamin Constant. Both parties deserve the name of "doctrinaires" only in this sense, that they have a "doctrine," a definite scheme of social and political reforms, whilst their opponents cherished, and still cherish, such vague expressions as "nationalism in the State" and "submission to popular ideals."

The writer owes a special debt of gratitude to Mrs. Birkbeck Hill, who most kindly undertook the ungrateful task of looking through his MS., and deleting or amending all that was contrary to the genius of the English language. Whatever measure of success this work may obtain will be largely due to Mrs. Hill.

MAXIME KOVALEVSKY.

*December* 1890.

# CONTENTS.

## LECTURE I.



## LECTURE II.



## LECTURE III.



## LECTURE IV.

## LECTURE V.



## LECTURE VI.

# MODERN CUSTOMS AND ANCIENT LAWS OF RUSSIA.

## LECTURE I.

### THE MATRIMONIAL CUSTOMS AND USAGES OF THE RUSSIAN PEOPLE, AND THE LIGHT THEY THROW ON THE EVOLUTION OF MARRIAGE.

The wide historical studies pursued by members of the University of Oxford necessarily include the study of the Slavonic race. The part which this race is beginning to play in the economic and social progress of our time, and the considerable achievements which it has already made in the fields of literature and science have attracted the attention even of those nations whose political interests are supposed not to coincide precisely with those of the Slavs. The Ilchester Lectures were, I believe, founded in order to make known to Oxford students the present and past of this undoubtedly Aryan branch of the human race. A good deal of work has already been done by my predecessors. Professor Thomson, of Copenhagen, by his careful study of the Norman origin of the Russian State, has greatly contributed to unveil even to Russians the mystery of their far-distant past, while Professor Turner, in the course of his brilliant lectures last year, made you acquainted with our best modern novelists. I do not know if my friend, the late Mr. W. R. S. Ralston, ever lectured in the Taylor Institute, but the accurate and lively accounts he has given of Russian epic poems and popular tales were undoubtedly written under the influence of the same feelings as those which inspired the founder of these lectures.

In England the works of Ralston were the first to deal with the vast field of Slavonic, and more especially of Russian, folk-lore. His chief endeavour was to show the great amount of information which the unwritten literature of Russia contains as to the early stages of religious development. But Russian folk-lore may interest a lawyer as well as a mythologist; its study may enrich comparative jurisprudence with new material not less than comparative mythology. It can no doubt unveil more than one mystery concerning the early state of European family law, and the various modes in which land was held by our remotest ancestors. The first stages in the history of political institutions, and more particularly the part which the common people were called upon in old days to play in the management of public affairs, can be illustrated by the history of Russian folk-motes and

Russian national councils, much better than by reference to the short notices left by Cæsar or Tacitus of the popular assemblies of the Germans. Russian serfdom, and the history of its abolition, may also be instructive in more than one point, even to those whose chief purpose is to study the origin, the growth, and the abolition of personal servitude in England, France, or Germany.

When I look to the great importance of the modern customs and ancient laws of Russia as regards the comparative history of institutions, I confidently hope to meet on your part with the indulgence which the lecturer needs who addresses his audience in a foreign tongue. I think that the study of Russian legal antiquities may to a certain extent be considered as a necessary appendage of those exhaustive inquiries in Indian and old Celtic institutions for which we are indebted to one of your most celebrated writers, the late Sir Henry Maine. I feel the more pleasure in mentioning his name, as it was by him that my first works in the field of comparative jurisprudence were inspired. His lectures have found readers in the remotest parts of the world, and have suggested to more than one foreign scholar the idea of re-writing the legal history of his own country.

Although recognising in him the chief representative of the legal school to which I belong, I shall more than once put forward theories which are altogether opposed to his: such an occasion presents itself at once in the study of early Russian family law.

This study will, I have no doubt, throw a clear light on the earliest period in the evolution of marriage—that of the matriarchate. I insist the more on this point because in England an opinion has been expressed that the customary law of Russia might be expected to give another illustration of the general prevalence of the patriarchal family even in the first stages of social development. Sir Henry Maine has more than once* expressed this opinion, and has found confirmation for it in certain quotations made chiefly from the well-known works of Haxthausen and Mackenzie Wallace. Both these authors, making a large use of the rich ethnographical literature of Russia, have correctly described the prevailing system of Russian joint families, or house communities, and their account may be taken generally as a good illustration of the old patriarchal family of the Germans and Celts. But neither of them had any opportunity of studying in detail the numerous survivals which we still find of a state of things which had nothing in common with agnatism, or even with a firmly established "patria potestas." Such was not, after all, the purpose that they had in view. Theirs was the study of contemporary life in Russian society, and the question of the primitive state of family relations in Russia cannot be settled

* The last time in an article on the patriarchal family published in the *Quarterly Review*.

by reference to works which do not deal with the subject.

Sir Henry Maine was also misled in his survey of Slavonic family law by the well-known Bohemian or Czech poem, "The Trial of the Princess Liubouscha." This poem he quotes at great length, and he states that it leaves no doubt as to the existence of a sort of undivided family or house-community in the most remote period of Bohemian history. Unfortunately, the poem on which he builds his conclusion is now unanimously declared both by Slavonic and German scholars to be a forgery by the well-known Bohemian philologist, Hanka. It is clear, therefore, that the whole of his theory, so far as it deals with Slavonic law and usage, is based either on facts which concern modern times alone, and have nothing to do with ancient times, or on documents manifestly false.

Now let us see what evidence we possess as to the character of early Slavonic family law. We shall first give our authorities, and then proceed to draw our general conclusions.

The earliest evidence which we possess as to the social relations of the Eastern Slavs, whose confederacy was the beginning of the Russian State, is contained in the so-called Chronicle of Nestor. Nestor is supposed to have been a Russian monk of the eleventh century.

Contrasting the mode of life of the most civilised Slavonic nation, the Polians, who were established on the banks of the Dnieper, with that of the more barbarous tribes of Russia, Nestor, or perhaps it is better to say, the unknown author of the Chronicle which bears this name, states as follows (I translate literally): "Each tribe had its own customs, and the laws of its forefathers and its own traditions, each its own manner of life (*nrav*). The Polians had the customs of their fathers, customs mild and peaceful (*tichi*); they showed a kind of reserve (*stidenie*) towards the daughters of their sons and towards their sisters, towards their mothers and their parents, towards the mothers of their wives, and towards the brothers of their husbands; to all of the persons named they showed great reserve. Amongst them the bridegroom did not go to seek his bride; she was taken to him in the evening, and the following morning they brought what was given for her."

"Another Slavonic tribe, the Drevlians, according to the same chronicler, lived like beasts; they killed one another, they fed on things unclean; no marriage took place amongst them, but they captured young girls on the banks of rivers."

The same author narrates that three other Slavonic tribes, the Radimich, the Viatich, and the Sever, had the same customs; they lived "in forests, like other wild animals, they ate everything unclean, and shameful things occurred amongst them between fathers and daughters-in-law. Marriages were unknown to them, but games were held in the outskirts of villages; they met at these games for dancing and every kind of diabolic amusement, and there they captured their wives, each man the one he had covenanted with. They had generally two or three wives."

I have tried to give you the nearest possible translation of this old Russian text, the interpretation of which, however, gives rise to certain difficulties not yet quite settled. I will now classify, to the best of my power, the various facts which we can infer from this text. First of all, it establishes the fact that marriage in the sense of a constant union between husband and wife, was not a general institution among the Eastern Slavs. With the exception of the more civilised Polians, no other tribe is stated to have any notion of it. Of course this does not mean that all alike were entirely ignorant of the meaning of family life. It only means that their mode of constituting a family did not correspond to the idea which the author, who, as we have said, was a monk, entertained as to matrimonial relations. The Radimich, Viatich, and Sever captured their wives after having previously come to an agreement with them. This certainly is a method which cannot meet with the approval of a a Christian, but nevertheless it is marriage. We have before us an example of what ethnologists have named "marriage by capture."

The Drevlians were even less advanced as regards the intercourse between the sexes. They also had games at which women were captured; but not a word is said about any covenant entered into by the captor and his supposed victim. Neither is any mention made of these games being held on the boundaries or outskirts of villages, a fact which would point to the existence of a sort of exogamy forbidding unions between persons of the same *gens*. In the description which the chronicler gives of the Drevlians we have an instance of an almost unlimited licence, whilst in that of the Radimich, Viatich and Sever we find a picture of an exogamous people; contracting marriage by capture, and yet retaining from the period of almost unlimited licence a sort of family communism which appears in the relations between fathers and daughters-in-law.

No trace of this either limited or unlimited promiscuousness is to be found among the Polians, who according to our old Chronicler, "conducted themselves with much reserve" towards daughters-in-law, and sisters-in-law, towards mothers and fathers, towards fathers-in-law and brothers-in-law. They seem to have been an exogamous tribe like the Radimich, Viatich and Sever, their wives being brought to them from outside their own *gens*. Unlike the tribes just mentioned they did not, however, procure them by capture. It was not the custom for the bridegrooms to go in search of their wives; they received them from the hands of the parents of the women, and they then paid the sum of money previously agreed upon. This means that their mode of constituting marriage was by buying their wives. The words of the Chronicler concerning these payments is far from being clear, and Russian scholars have tried to interpret them in the sense of "dower" brought by the relatives of the wife. But it has been recently proved that no mention of "dower" is to be found in Russian charters before the fifteenth century, and that the word *veno* used in mediæval Russian to designate the payment made on marriage, has no other meaning than that of *pretium nuptiale,* or payment made by the bridegroom to the family of the bride.* The words of Tacitus concerning the *dos* paid amongst the German tribes by the future husband to his wife's father give precisely the meaning of the old Russian *veno,* and throw a light on the sort of payment which the chronicle of Nestor had in view, when speaking of the matrimonial customs of the Polians.

The testimony of our oldest Chronicle concerning the different forms of matrimony among the eastern Slavs deserves our closest attention, because it is, in all points, confirmed by the study of the rest of our old written literature, of our epic poems, of our wedding-songs, and of the matrimonial usages and customs still or lately in existence in certain remote districts of Russia. The Drevlians are not the only Slavonic tribe to which the mediæval chronicles

* Compare Lange, "On the Mutual Rights, according to Old Russian Law, of Husband and Wife as regards Fortune." Petersburg, 1886.

ascribe a low state of morality. The same is asserted of the old Bohemians or Czechs in the account given of their manners and customs by Cosmas of Prague, a Latin annalist of the eleventh century, who says: *Connubia erant illis communia. Nam more pecudum singulas ad noctes novos probant hymenaeos, et surgente aurora . . . . ferrea amoris rumpunt vincula.*" This means: "They practised communal marriage. For, like animals, they contracted each night a fresh marriage, and as soon as the dawn appeared they broke the iron bonds of love."

This statement is directly confirmed by that of another mediæval author, the unknown biographer of St. Adalbert. This writer ascribes the animosity of the Bohemian people towards the saint to the fact of his strong opposition to the shameful promiscuity which in his time prevailed in Bohemia. It is confirmed, also, by the monk of the Russian Abbey of Eleasar, known by the name of Pamphil, who lived in the sixteenth century. Both speak of the existence of certain yearly festivals at which great licence prevailed. According to the last-named author, such meetings were regularly held on the borders of the State of Novgorod on the banks of rivers, resembling, in that particular, the annual festivals mentioned by Nestor. Not later than the beginning of the sixteenth century, they were complained of by the clergy of the State of Pscov. It was at that time that Pamphil drew up his letter to the Governor of the State, admonishing him to put an end to these annual gatherings, since their only result was the corruption of the young women and girls. According to the author just cited, the meetings took place, as a rule, the day before the festival of St. John the Baptist, which, in pagan times, was that of a divinity known by the name of Jarilo, corresponding to the Priapus of the Greeks. Half a century later the new ecclesiastical code, compiled by an assembly of divines convened in Moscow by the Czar Ivan the Terrible, took effectual measures for abolishing every vestige of paganism; amongst them, the yearly festivals held on Christmas Day, on the day of the baptism of our Lord, and on St. John the Baptist, commonly called Midsummer Day. A general feature of all these festivals, according to the code, was the prevalence of the promiscuous intercourse of the sexes. How far the clergy succeeded in suppressing these yearly meetings, which had been regularly held for centuries before on the banks of rivers, we cannot precisely say, although the fact of their occasional occurrence, even in modern times, does not tend to prove their complete abolition. More than once have I had an opportunity of being present at these nightly meetings, held at the end of June, in commemoration of a heathen divinity. They usually take place close to a river or pond; large fires are lighted, and over them young couples, bachelors and unmarried girls, jump barefoot. I have never found any trace of licentiousness; but there is no doubt that cases of licence do occur, though seldom in our time. That a few centuries ago they were very frequent has been lately proved by some curious documents preserved in the archives of some of the provincial ecclesiastical councils, particularly in those existing in the Government of Kharkov. According to these documents, the local clergy were engaged in constant warfare with the shameful licentiousness which prevailed at the evening assembles of the peasants, and more than once the clergy succeeded in inducing the authorities of the village to dissolve the assemblies by force. The priests were often wounded, and obliged to seek refuge in the houses of the village elders from the stones with which they were pelted. These evening assemblies are known to the people of Great Russia under the name of *Posidelki*, and to the Little Russians by that of *Vechernitzi*.

The licentiousness which formed the characteristic feature of these meetings throws light on the motives which induce the peasants of certain Great Russian communes to attach but small importance to virginity. Russian ethnographers have not infrequently mentioned the fact of young men living openly with unmarried women, and, even in case of marriage, of giving preference to those who were known to have already been mothers.

However peculiar all these facts may seem, they are very often met with among people of quite a distinct race. The Allemanic populations of the Grisons, no longer ago than the sixteenth century, held regular meetings which were not less shameful than those of the Cossacks. The *Kilbenen* were abolished by law,* but another custom, in direct antagonism to morality, continued to exist all over the northern cantons of Switzerland and in the southern provinces of Wurtemberg and of Baden. I mean the custom known under the name of *Kirchgang* or *Dorfgehen*, which, according to the popular songs, consisted in nothing else than the right of a bachelor to become the lover of some young girl, and that quite openly, and with the implied consent of the parents of his sweetheart. May I also mention a similar custom amongst the Welsh, known as "bundling"? I am not well enough informed as to the character of this custom to insist on its resemblance to those already mentioned. The little I have said on the German survivals of early licence may suffice to establish this general conclusion: that the comparative immorality of Russian peasants has no other cause than the survival amongst them of numerous vestiges of the early forms of marriage.

Another feature of the matriarchal family, the lack of any prohibition as to marriages between persons who are sprung from the same father or grandfather, is also mentioned more than once by early Slavonic writers. Such marriages were not prohibited by custom among the old Bohemians or Czechs. "Populus miscebatur cum cognatis," says the biographer of St. Adalbert. They are also frequently mentioned

* "Das Landrecht von Kloster," (XVIc.) ed. by Mohr.

in the epic poems of our peasants, the so-called *bilini*, of which the late W. R. S. Ralston has given to English readers an accurate and profound analysis. I will quote certain passages from these poems to give you the facts on which my theory is based.

One of the most celebrated heroes of our popular ballads, Ilia Mourometz, encounters one day a freebooter named Nightingale (Solovei Razboinik). "Why," asks the hero, "do all thy children look alike?" Nightingale gives the following answer: "Because, when my son is grown up, I marry him to my daughter; and when my daughter is old enough, I give her my son for a husband, and I do so in order that my race may not die out." Another popular ballad, representing the evil customs of former days, describes them in the following manner:

> Brother made war upon brother,
> Brother took sister to wife.

Endogamous marriages still occur in a few very remote parts of Russia. Such is the case in certain villages in the district of Onega, and especially in that of Liamika, where the peasants do their best to infringe the canonical prescriptions which disallow marriage between blood relations to the fourth degree inclusively. The same has also been noticed in certain parts of the Government of Archangel, quite on the shores of the White Sea, where the peasants are in the habit of saying that marriages between blood relations will be blessed with a more rapid increase of "cattle"—the word "cattle" standing in this case for *children*. In some provinces of Siberia and in the district of Vetlouga, which belongs to the Government of Nijni Novgorod, endogamous marriages, though contrary to the prevailing custom are looked upon with a favourable eye.*

Another fact, which deserves the attention of all partisans of the theory of the matriarchate, first promulgated by McLennan, is, the large independence enjoyed by the Slavonic women of old days. Let me first quote the words of Cosmas of Prague, which relate to this subject, and then show you what illustration they find both in written literature, and in popular ballads and songs.

Non virgines viri, sed ipsœmet viros, quos et quando voluerunt, accipiebant.

Such is the statement of Cosmas Pragensis, (ch. xxi). This means: "It is not the men who choose the maids, but the maids themselves who take the husbands they like, and when they like."

This freedom of the Bohemian girls to dispose of their hearts according to their own wish shows the comparative independence of the Bohemian women at that period.

The oldest legal code of this people, the *sniem*, seems to favour this independence by recognising the right of the women to be free from any work, except

---

* Smirnov, "Sketches of Family Relations according to the Customary Law of the Russians" (Moscow, 1877), pp. 105, 106.

that which is connected with the maintenance of the household.*

Confronted with the facts just brought forward, the popular legend, reported by Cosmas in his chronicle, of a kind of Bohemian Amazons, who took an active part in the wars of the time, appears in its true light. Free as they were from the bonds of marriage, not relying on husbands for the defence of their persons and estates, the old Bohemian Amazons were probably very similar to those warlike women who still appear in the King of Dahomey's army, and who in the time of Pompey were known to exist among certain autochthonic tribes of the Caucasus. A fact well worth notice is that the memory of these bellicose women is still preserved in the traditions of the Tcherkess, who call them by the name of "emcheck." Giantesses, wandering by themselves through the country and fighting the heroes they meet on their way, are also mentioned more than once in our popular ballads, or *bilini.* The name under which they are known is that of *polinitzi,* the word *pole* meaning the field and in a secondary sense the battle-field.

Like the Bohemian girls described by Cosmas of Prague, these Russian Amazons chose their lovers as they liked.

"Is thy heart inclined to amuse itself with me?"

* Ivanischev, "Dissertation on the Rights of the Individual according to the Old Laws of the Bohemians." Complete Works, p. 92.

such is the question addressed to Ilia Mourometz by one of these Amazons, the so-called Beautiful Princess. "Be my husband and I will be thy wife," says another of these *polinitzi*, Anastasia the Beautiful, to the paladin, Theodor Tougarin. It is not the freebooter Nightingale who chooses his wife, nor the paladin Dobrinia who is going in search of a bride; both are represented as accepting the offers of betrothal made to them by the Russian Amazons, Zaprava and Marina.*

Evidence of still greater importance is that of the French writer, Beauplan, who, speaking of the manners and customs of the inhabitants of Little Russia during his time, the latter half of the seventeenth century, states as follows:

"In the Ukraine, contrary to the custom of all other nations, the husbands do not choose their wives, but are themselves chosen by their future consorts."

I hope I have now given an amount of information sufficient to answer the purpose I have in view; which is no other, than to show that, in a low state of morality, communal marriage between near relations and endogamy, went hand in hand amongst the early Slavs with a considerable degree of independence among the weaker sex.

To all these characteristic features of the matri-

* Ribnikov, "The Songs of the Russian People," vol. i. p. 64. Kirscha Danilov, "Old Russian Poems," pp. 9 and 70. Afanasiev, "Tales of the Russian People," vol. i. p. 484.

archate we may add this very important one, that, according to the old Russian law, the tie which unites a man to his sister and the children she has brought into the world, was considered to be closer than that which unites two brothers or the uncle and his nephew. In a society organised on the principle of agnatism, the son of a sister has no reason to interfere in the pursuit of the murderer of his uncle. The brother belongs altogether to another clan, and the duty of vengeance falls exclusively on the persons of that clan. But such is by no means the point of view of the old Russian law, recognising, as it does, the right of the sister's son to avenge the death of his uncle.

"In case a man shall be killed by a man," decrees the first article of the Pravda of Yaroslav (the *lex barborum* of the Russians), "vengeance may be taken by a son, in case his father has been killed; by the father, when the son falls a victim; by the brother's son and by the son of a sister." These last words are omitted in the later versions of the Pravda, a fact which shows the increase of agnatic organisation, but they are found in the version generally recognised as the most ancient.

This close tie between brother and sister, between the uncle and the sister's children, still exists among the Southern Slavs. Professor Bogisic, and after him Mr. Krauss, have illustrated this fact by the epic songs of the Servian people. They speak of the custom generally in use among the Southern Slavs of securing from a person truthfulness in his statements by the invocation of the name of the sister. They mention, too, that peculiar relation of artificial brotherhood and sisterhood, into which young men and young women belonging to different kindreds frequently enter, in order to secure to the weaker sex protection and help.

I hardly need insist on the importance which all these facts have with regard to the theory of an early matriarchate among the Slavs, the more so because this has already been done in England by Mr. McLennan, in his well-known study on the Patriarchal theory, and in Germany by Bachofen in one of his Antiquarian Letters.* But I shall complete the information which these scholars have given by citing certain peculiar customs still in use among Russian peasants.

Whilst the father is considered to be the proper person to dispose of the hand of the bride, the brother, according to the wedding ritual, appears as the chief protector of her virginity. In more than one province of Russia the brother plays an important part in that portion of the nuptial ceremony which may be called by the Latin name of *in domus deductio*. As soon as the bridegroom has made his appearance in the court-yard of the family to which his bride belongs, the brother, in accordance with an old custom, takes his seat next the bride with a

* "Antiquarische Briefe," 1880, p. 167. McLennan, "The Patriarchal Theory," ch. vi. p. 71.

naked sword, or at least a stick, in his hand. The bridegroom, or the groomsman, asking to be allowed to take his seat, receives as answer, that the brother is there to keep ward over his sister, and that he will not consent to leave his seat unless he be paid for it. "Dear brother, don't give me away for nothing. Ask a hundred roubles for me, for the veil which covers my head a thousand roubles. Ask for my beauty—God alone knows how much" Such is the tenor of the song composed for the occasion. "The brother, a true Tartar," we read in the text of another nuptial song, "has sold his sister for a thaler, and her fair tresses for fifty copecks."

In Little Russia the drawn sword which the brother holds in his hand on the occasion is ornamented with the red berries of the guelder-rose, red being the emblem of maidenhood among Slavonic peoples. Other emblems are the binding of the bride's tresses, and the veil which covers her head. The bridegroom is not allowed to remove the veil, nor to unbind the tresses of his future wife, unless he consents to pay a small sum of money to her brother.

Hitherto we have considered the different aspects of the earliest period in the evolution of the family—that which is known by the term of the matriarchate. The various features which characterised the lowest state of the relations between the sexes did not vanish all at once. The incestuous relations between persons of the same blood seem to have been the first to disappear. No further mention of these occurs in Nestor's description of the Eastern tribes—the Radimich, Viatich, and Sever. Though they practise communal marriage so far that fathers and sons have wives in common, nevertheless fathers and daughters, brothers and sisters, dare no longer cohabit with each other, and if licence still occurs at some annual festivities, it is kept under some check.

The *bilini*, or popular ballads, as also the old legends and folk tales, often represent that transient period of social evolution, when endogamy was gradually giving way to exogamy, and relations between persons of the same kin were forbidden. A popular hero, known by the name of Michailo Kasarinov, and belonging to a later series of Russian paladins, in one of these ballads liberates a young Russian girl from the yoke of the Tartars, and is on the point of becoming her lover, when she discloses to him the secret of her birth, and proves that she is his sister. The paladin immediately abandons his purpose. In another popular tale, inserted by Afanasiev in his collection of these curious monuments of our unwritten literature, a brother is represented as insisting on marrying his sister, and the latter as strongly protesting against his desire. "What do you propose to do?" she asks. "Bethink you of God and of the sin? Is it right that a brother should espouse his own sister?" The brother persists, and the couple are on the point of retiring when the earth opens, and the sister, unharmed, disappears from view.* In another popular legend, a husband, having discovered that his wife is his own sister, finds no means of escape but that of undertaking a pilgrimage in order to expiate his sins.†

The prohibition is gradually extended to all persons of the same kin. A song ‡ in vogue among the peasantry of Little Russia speaks of a bird wishing to marry, and finding no bride at his birthplace, all the females being his relations, there remains nothing for him to do but to cross the sea, and seek a bride of another kin than his own.

The complete discomfiture of endogamy in its long struggle with exogamous prescriptions is shown in the fact that in some parts of Russia, as for instance in the government of Simbirsk, in certain villages of the government of Olonizk, and of the district of Schadrinsk, inhabited by the Cosacks of the Don, the bride is always taken from another village than the bridegroom's. Even in provinces in which no similar custom is known to exist, the remembrance of the time when exogamy was considered a duty, is preserved in the fact that the bridegroom is constantly spoken of as a foreigner (*choujoy, choujaninin*), and his friends and attendants are represented as coming with him from a distant country, in order to take away the future spouse.

---

* Afanasiev, "Folk-tales," vol. i. pp. 211, 212.

† Schein, "Songs of the White Russians."

‡ Tereschenko, "Social Life of the Russians," vol. iv. p. 280.

The origin of exogamy has been sought for in the fact of the general prevalence, at a certain period of social development, of the custom of capturing wives. The co-existence of both customs has been already noticed by the old Russian chronicler in his description of the manners and customs of the Radimich, Viatich, and Sever. His testimony is corroborated by that of the nuptial songs, and of the ceremonies still in use at country weddings. The information which is derived from these sources as to the general prevalence in past times of marriage by capture, I have summed up in a work published in Russian under the title of "The first Periods in the Evolution of Law." I shall take the liberty of bringing forward to-day the facts there summarised. They concern the Eastern as well as the Southern Slavs.

Amongst the Southern Slavs, marriage by capture was still in existence no longer ago than the beginning of the present century. A well-known Servian writer, Vouk Karadjich, gives the following details about this peculiar custom, known under the name of *otmitza*. "The capture of girls in order to marry them is still practised among the Servians. Young men very frequently have recourse to this mode of procuring a wife. On such occasions they are equipped and armed as if they were going out to do battle. They conceal themselves, and quietly await the moment till the girl passes near them on her way to look after the cattle. Sometimes they make a direct attack on the homestead she inhabits.

In either case her resistance has no other result than a direct appeal to physical force. The young men seize her by her long plaited tresses, drag and push her along, and sometimes use a whip or a stick to quicken her pace. The same custom prevailed not long ago in Montenegro. It existed also for centuries in Croatia, as may be seen from the mention made of it in the statute of Politza, a legal code published in 1605. In Bosnia and Herzegovina abductions still occur, but, as a rule, with the previous consent of the supposed victim, and with the declared intention of avoiding the expenses of a regular betrothal."

So much as regards marriage among the Southern Slavs.

As to the Eastern Slavs, the early development of a strong government, and of a powerful clergy, prevented the possibility of a long continuance of this wild method of constituting a family. An exception must, however, be made as regards the Cosacks of Little Russia and the Ukraine; who, according to the statement of Beauplan, continued to capture their wives no longer ago than the seventeenth century. But the existence, probably in Pagan times, of marriage by capture in Russia, as well as in Poland, is still revealed by the old ballads, the wedding ceremonies of the country people, and the songs in use on the occasion of a betrothal.

The *bilini* more than once mention the cases of paladins like Ilia Mourometz having a personal encounter with the Amazons they meet on their way. As soon as the paladins have succeeded in vanquishing the Amazons, they force them to become their wives. Among the different ceremonies still in use at a country wedding, one particularly deserves our attention, on account of the symbolical representation of the means to which the family of the bride once had recourse to prevent an abduction. On the day fixed for the wedding the doors leading to the homestead of the bride are closely shut. Sometimes a temporary wooden wall is erected to preserve the family from intrusion. The wedding-songs still in use in the Government of Toula speak of the necessity of defending the approach to the bride's residence by oak trees, cut down to block up the road, and by shields arranged before the principal entrance of the homestead.

The bridegroom and his friends wear a warlike dress; they are mounted on horseback, and carry guns and pistols. Such, at least, is the custom in the western provinces of Russia, whilst in the southern the whip, carried by the bridegroom's best man, appears to be the only weapon in use. The wedding-songs speak of arrows, shot in the direction of the bride's home, and of stone walls broken down, in order to take possession of her. The bridegroom and his followers are regularly met like foes. In the Government of Perm it is the custom for the father of the bride to fire a pistol over their heads, of course a pistol charged only with powder. The same custom is also in use in certain parts of the Government of

Archangel. The wedding-song speaks of the bridegroom's train in the following terms:

> They will come to the maiden's father
> With war.
> They will rob him,
> And imprison the mother.
> They will take the young girl away
> To a strange land.

But capture, as we have already seen, was not the only mode of contracting marriage among the Slavs, even in the earliest period. According to the chronicle of Nestor, the Polians never had recourse to it. Instead of carrying off his bride by force, the Polian bridegroom preferred to pay to her father, or her family, a sort of *pretium nuptiale*, or bride-price. This custom of the Polians gradually became the general usage among all Slavonic tribes. In Servia, according to Vouk Karadjich, the sums of money paid to the bride's father by the bridegroom's family were so exorbitant that Georgius the Black issued a proclamation declaring it to be illegal to ask from the bridegroom more than a single ducat. In our days, says Bogisic, wives, as a rule, cannot be bought by their future husbands, but a reminiscence of this old custom is still preserved in the fact that the bride's father receives from the bridegroom a gift in money, varying from one to six ducats, according to the fortune of the giver.

Wives were also bought and sold among the Slavonic tribes of Austria. According to an old usage of the Loujichan, a Slavonic people inhabiting certain districts of Hungary, the bridegroom, on entering the homestead of his bride, apostrophised the father thus: "Pray do tell me if you have a cow to sell?" A Bohemian wedding-song puts into the mouth of the bridegroom's best man the following sentence: "Please deliver to me the bride. I will give you a good price for her. The only reason I have for being here is that I may pay you in heavy thalers." No longer ago than the beginning of the last century, young men wishing to marry were in the habit of going to the fair at Krasni Brod, where unmarried women and widows, surrounded by their relations, awaited their coming. Each chose the woman he liked best, covenanted with her parents as to the amount of money to be paid for her, and proceeded to the ceremony of marriage. Polish wedding-songs also mention the custom of buying wives.

In Posnau the following ceremony is still observed on the occasion of a betrothal: The bridegroom puts a small piece of money on the shoes of his bride, another on her knee, a third on her shoulder, a fourth on her head. It is only when this ceremony has been performed that the father delivers the maiden into the hands of her future husband.

I have already mentioned the fact that the payment made in Old Russia by the bridegroom was known under the name of *veno*. The true meaning of this word is revealed by the use which is made of it by the translators of the Scriptures. In a Slavonic version of the words addressed by Jacob to Laban, when he asked him for the hand of his daughter Rachel, the translators write as follows: Increase the sum of the *veno* as much as you like and I will pay it to you, and you shall give me this maiden to wife.*

In modern times the *veno* is mentioned only in certain wedding songs. Another term, *kladka,* has replaced it in most parts of Great Russia. This payment, amounting in certain parts of Russia to the sum of one hundred, and even of two or three hundred roubles, is made to the father of the bride. As a rule, the father disposes of the money in favour of his daughter, for he gives her as dowry a larger or smaller sum, according to what he has received from the bridegroom. But this fact cannot be brought forward as a proof that the *kladka* belongs by right to the bride. In more than one commune of the Government of Tambov, Riasan, Vladimir, Moscow, Samara and Saratov, no mention is made of the dowry given by the bride's father, whilst the *kladka* is regularly paid to the head of the family to which the bride belongs.† We must therefore consider these two payments, that made by the bridegroom, and that made by the bride's father, as quite different institutions. The one payment proves the existence, at least in certain parts of modern Russia, of a mode of marriage similar to that

---

* Genesis xxix.

† Lange, p. 86.

of the Indian *Asura,* the other shows the way in which the *pretium emptionis,* to employ a term of Roman jurisprudence, passed into the *dos* or dowry. The custom was the same as that followed by the Germanic tribes. In saying this I have particularly in view Tacitus's statement about the payment made by the bridegroom at a marriage, and the more recent fact of the conversion of this payment into a dowry given by the bride's father.

That in former days in Russia wives were regularly bought from their parents is plainly recognised by the wedding-songs still in use among our peasants.

The *boyars,* a term by which people designate the companions or followers of the bridegroom, who on his part is called "the duke," *kniaz,* the *boyars,* says a wedding-song of the Government of Saratov, "surround the yard of the bride's house on all sides; they bargain for our Douniascha."

"The *boyars* have covered the ground with gold," sing the country people of White Russia.

The bridegroom is very often mentioned in the songs of the peasants of Great Russia as the "merchant," whilst the bride is spoken of as "merchandise." In the Government of Jaroslav, for instance, the bride, following an ancient usage, complains of the treatment to which she will be subjected, saying that "unknown merchants will take her away from her father and her dear mother."*

* Titov, "Customary Village Law." Nicola Perevos in the District of Rostov (Jaroslav, 1888), Appendix N. 5.

Now that we have carefully passed in review the different aspects under which matrimonial relations have been viewed, or still are viewed, by the country people of Russia, we may be allowed to say, that Russian ethnography quite corroborates the theory as to the evolution of marriage which English scholars were the first to establish. The author of "Primitive Culture," as well as the great and powerful genius who has so marvellously continued the work of Auguste Comte, and lastly the numerous followers of the man, whose studies in ancient history have unveiled for us the mysteries of the early family, will, I have no doubt, be pleased to see their views confirmed by the early law and the still living custom of one of the principal branches of the Aryan race. Nothing more, it seems to me, is wanting to the modern theory of the matriarchate than a solid base of historical facts. So long as obscure myths and the more or less superficial observations of missionaries and tourists constituted the materials for a theory whose chief purpose is to show us the social state of our most remote ancestors, objections like those of Sir Henry Maine or Mr. Starcke found a ready ear. The fact that among the Kamilaroi and the Kurnai the right of the husband is ignored, does not necessarily imply that our ancestors had no notion of marriage and the *patria potestas;* and the numerous Greek myths on which Bachofen has established his hypothesis of any early Greek gyneocracy may possibly belong to the number of those wandering legends on which it is very difficult to found an opinion as to the social state of this or that particular people.

Consult the "Sociology" of Herbert Spencer, and especially the chapters in which he treats of the early forms of marriage, and you will, I am sure, be surprised at the discovery that scarcely any mention is made of the legal antiquities of peoples belonging to the Aryan race. This is a serious defect, and the sooner it is remedied the better. Some measures have already been taken to this end by the modern school of German jurists who, under the able guidance of Professor Köhler, publish a most interesting periodical called the *Zeitschrift fur die vergleichende Rechtswissenschaft.* It is with an object similar to theirs that I have undertaken my researches in the vast field of Slavonic law and custom. What I have said about it in this lecture, little though it has been, may, perchance, induce some of you to undertake fresh studies in this region which is still so little explored. I can promise all who will venture, the most abundant and happy results.

## LECTURE II.

### THE STATE OF THE MODERN RUSSIAN FAMILY, AND PARTICULARLY THAT OF THE JOINT OR HOUSEHOLD COMMUNITY OF GREAT RUSSIA.

We believe that the theory of the matriarchate finds a solid basis in the past history of the Russian family. The present condition of the latter seems to prove that the next stage in its evolution was the household community, composed of persons united by descent from a common forefather and accompanied by that worship of ancestors which usually resulted from it. The complete subjection of the wife to the husband, and of the children to the father; community of goods and the common enjoyment of their produce by the relatives living under the same roof; the acknowledged superiority of old age and of direct descent from the common ancestor; the total absence of testamentary dispositions of property, and even of that mode of legal succession which supposes partition, and the exclusion of the more remote by the nearer kin; the elimination of women from participation in the family estate because marriage makes them aliens; all these features of the patriarchal family so ably illustrated in the works of Sir Henry Maine, reappear in the modern constitution of the Russian family. I mean, of course, that of the country people, the middle and higher classes having already adopted European manners and customs, and being on that account subjected to a legislation which, on more than one point, is in direct opposition to customary law.

Let us study one by one the characteristic features of this family constitution of the peasant, a constitution more like that of the early Celts and Germans than that of any of the modern nations of Europe.

The great importance still attached by the Russian peasant to agnatism, that is to relationship on the father's side, is shown by the part which ancestor worship plays even now at the celebration of a country wedding. Before becoming a member of her husband's family, the bride must sever all the ties which have hitherto bound her to the house-spirits under whose protection she has passed her youth, and must solemnly adopt the worship of those of the family into which she is about to enter. This public manifestation of a change of worship is most clearly seen in the wedding ceremonies of the Southern Slavs. It is not so distinctly preserved in those of the Eastern Slavs. Both these races being identical as to their origin and nature, I will begin by first stating the religious customs, customs of an undoubtedly pagan origin—still in use at Bulgarian betrothals. "In Lika," says M. Bogisic, "the bride, before leaving her father's house, goes three times round the hearth, prostrating herself each time, as if to implore forgiveness." As you are aware of the intimate connection which has existed between the worship of the hearth and that of the family ancestors, I need not tell you that the act performed by the Bulgarian bride before leaving her parent's house has no other meaning than that of a last invocation of the house-spirits whose worship she is on the point of abandoning.

The spirits are supposed to be hurt by the decision she has taken to withdraw to her husband's homestead, and to be appeased by an act of humiliation on her part. When she is once in the bridegroom's house the maiden is obliged to perform another ceremony; she must seat herself close to the hearth, in order to keep up for a short time the fire burning thereon by pieces of wood thrown on to it with her own hands. The symbolical character of this ceremony may easily be perceived. The young wife is on the point of becoming a member of the house community of her husband, and as such, a participant in its family worship. Her acquiescence must be expressed by a symbol, and her keeping up the fire on the hearth is precisely such a symbol. The custom just described exists all over Bulgaria and has been more than once alluded to by modern ethnographers, M. Bogisic, Mr. Krauss, and others.

Let us now examine the corresponding customs of the Russian peasantry. In little Russia the bride, while her father is discussing the question of her marriage with the person sent by the bridegroom, is obliged by custom to remain near the hearth, towards which she stretches out her hand. By so doing she expresses her desire still to remain under the protection of the house-spirits of her family, the so-called "domovoi." A century ago, according to the statement of Kalinovsky, the day on which the bride was taken to the house of her future husband, a great fire was lighted in the yard before it, and the young couple were obliged to cross it sitting in their carriage. This custom is still observed in certain parts of the Government of Kiev, but only in those cases in which the bride is known to have misbehaved before marriage. Heaps of straw are kindled on such occasions in the yard before the bridegroom's house, and the bride who has passed safely over these fires is considered to be purified. But this does not prevent her, as soon as she has entered the house of her husband, from seeking refuge at the hearth, where she stands for a while singing a carol, the meaning of which is that she laments her past bad conduct and promises to be a good wife.

I beg you to observe that the fires are lighted in the yard of the bridegroom's house and that they are to be considered as being in direct relation with the house-community to which he belongs. Not every fire has the power of purification, only that which represents the family hearth. It is to this hearth that the young wife appeals for protection, should she have any reason to fear any ill-treatment from her husband's family, on account of her former conduct; it is before this hearth that she confesses and repents and promises to be a good and faithful wife.

In a society, in which the interests of the family constantly prevail over those of the individual (and such is certainly the case in all patriarchal societies, and amongst them the Russian), there is no room for marriages contracted by the mutual consent of the young people. I do not mean to say that Russian parents, whose duty it is to find suitable matches for their sons and daughters, never take into account the feelings of those they intend to unite. I wish only to impress on you the idea that they are not obliged to do so by custom. On more than one occasion Russian customary courts have plainly expressed the opinion that a marriage contract concluded by the bride's father with that of the future husband is a legal act, for the infringement of which amends ought to be made by the restitution to the party wronged of the loss he or she may have sustained.

The clergy very early endeavoured to put an end to the arbitrary manner in which parents disposed of their children's future, but the force of custom and the feeling that supported it were so strong that the only measure which the ecclesiastical statute of Jaroslav (XIth century) introduced for the protection of the freedom of marriageable children was the one by which a fine which went to the bishop was inflicted on the parents of a daughter who, after a marriage contracted against her will, had committed suicide.

The country people still believe that a marriage without the parent's approval will call down the wrath of Heaven on the heads of the young couple. This moral sanction, the right of parents to decide the future of their children, has received from the customary law of Russia the support of a penalty in case of disobedience; the son and daughter who conclude a marriage without consulting their parents, lose all rights to inheritance and dowry.

According to modern Russian law, marriage is a religious act; it cannot be performed without the help of the Church, and is regarded as a sacrament. But such is by no means the light in which the country people look on it, nor was it the view of the old Russian law. For many centuries the Russian clergy had to fight against the inveterate custom of our lower classes to contract unions without the sanction of the Church. The young couple saved the expense of a religious ceremony and thought their union legally established as soon as they were publicly joined to each other in the presence of the community, which was invited on the occasion to a sort of festival called the *vesselic.* No later than the end of the sixteenth century an assembly of Divines convened by Ivan the Cruel entered a strong protest against the custom which everywhere prevailed of omitting the religious consecration of the marriage tie, and strong measures were in consequence taken against those who did not comply with the requirements of the clergy. All, however, failed, and marriage remained in the eyes of the common people nothing more than a sort of civil contract, entered into in the presence of the community as a sign of its recognition and sanction.

That such generally was, and still is, the prevailing opinion of the Russian peasant may be seen from the following facts.

Among the Cossacks of the Don, not more than a century ago, people, as a general rule, were joined in marriage in the following way: The young couple, after previous agreement, went to the popular assembly of the village, or stanitza, this assembly being known by the name of *Majdan*, and declared that they had made up their minds to become husband and wife. "Be my wife," said the bridegroom to the bride. "Be my husband," she answered. "So be it," chanted the assembly. "We wish you good luck and happiness.*

On the Don the absence of a religious ceremony may, to a certain extent, be explained by the scarcity of priests; but such is by no means the case in those provinces which were annexed to Muscovy in the middle of the seventeenth century, after ages of political dependence on Poland. I refer to the Governments of Kiev, Tchernigov, and Poltava, which

* Charousin, "The Cossack Communities of the Don" (Moscow, 1885), p. 74.

constitute what in our days is known under the name of Little Russia. It is, therefore, very interesting to find that in those provinces the religious consecration of marriage is still considered by the peasants as a superfluous ceremony. Matrimonial life begins here after the nuptial festival, the "vesselic," and weeks may pass before the couple find it necessary to be married at church. Facts of the same description have been noticed by Madame Efimenko in the extreme north of Russia, in the Government of Archangel, occupied by colonists from Great Russia.

The customary law of Russia, like the old German jurisprudence, established a difference between betrothal and marriage. Both are considered to be legal acts, and both ought therefore to have distinct legal effects. Betrothal is legally concluded as soon as the two families have come to an agreement, first, as to the amount of the marriage expenses each party is to bear, and secondly, as to the time fixed for the wedding. The expenses are of different kinds: they comprise, first, the "kladka" of the bridegroom, a sort of *pretium emptionis* paid to the bride's father, and the dowry which the bride receives from her family. Then come the presents to be made by each party to the parents of the bride and those of the bridegroom, and the amount of expense which the bridegroom has to incur on the occasion of the nuptial feast. All these are regularly discussed and settled by a sort of verbal agreement, known among the peasantry by the name of "riad." In ancient Russia when agreements of this kind were entered into even by the higher classes, the "riad" was always put down in the form of a written contract, and this is still occasionally done in the northern Governments of Russia, especially in that of Archangel. Betrothal is considered to be legally concluded at the moment when the two parties, that of the bridegroom and that of the bride, have shaken hands. It is not without reason that I insist on the fact that it is this indefinite expression of the two parties which concludes the act of betrothal. I want to impress on your minds that the presence of the bridegroom's father is not considered necessary. An outsider, called "Svat," may be authorised by the father to speak and act for him in a contract of this sort.

As soon as the ceremony of shaking hands is over neither of the contracting parties can break the engagement without incurring the obligation of pecuniary compensation for the wrong he does to the other party by his breach of contract. This compensation is of two different kinds: the one seems to have rather a moral, the other a purely monetary or material origin. If the bride's party breaks the contract, the bridegroom and his family consider themselves injured in their honour. If, however, the breach of promise has been made by the bridegroom, the case is more serious. Then it is not only the honour of the bride that suffers, but also the material interests of the family, since a bride rejected by the man whom she was on the point of marrying, will generally experience great difficulty in finding another suitor. Such being the case, the customary court of the village usually accords to the party aggrieved the right to demand a pecuniary compensation "for the loss of honour the bride is supposed to have sustained" ("sa beschestic," say our peasants). In case security has been received for a bridegroom's performance of his promise by a pledge or by the partial payment of the money which he owes to the bride's father, the question of compensation is easily settled, as the family of the bride retain for her own use the money already received; but if no payment has been made, the court must decide the amount to be paid. It very seldom happens that the sum demanded exceeds thirty roubles, at least, in the provinces of Great Russia. No extenuating circumstances are admitted on this occasion by the Court. A father having once declared that he was drunk when he gave his consent to the proposed marriage of his son, received no other answer but this: "You may be drunk, but you must be clever" (будь пьянъ да уменъ).

The breach of contract may have two different results: one, that which I have just mentioned, a compensation in money for the loss of honour; as to the other, I have already stated that the contract of betrothal contains certain engagements as to the amount of the *pretium emptionis*, of the dowry and of the different expenses to be incurred by each party on the occasion of the marriage. If certain of these engagements have been partly fulfilled before the breach of promise, the wronged party has the right to demand the restitution of the money which had been spent; the bridegroom receives back the presents which he has made to his bride, and the bride those given to the bridegroom. The Courts uniformly recognise the necessity for such mutual restitution, the only exception being when the money already paid serves to constitute the amount of compensation to either party for the wrong inflicted by the loss of honour.

The contract of marriage which follows that of betrothal, cannot at the present time be dissolved; but we should be mistaken if we inferred from this fact that this indissolubility of marriage has always been recognised by the common law of Russia. Though the peasants are now known to use the following aphorisms: "Marriage is known but not unmarriage;" "A bad pope may marry you, but even a good one cannot unmarry you," the case was quite different in the past. Not longer ago than the end of the eighteenth century the Cossacks of the Don practiced divorce. A husband and wife who did not wish to live together any longer, appeared before the popular assembly and made the following declaration: "This woman is no longer my wife;" "this man is no longer my husband." "Be it so," was the answer of the assembly, and the marriage tie ceased to exist. During the sixteenth century husbands in Great Russia were still accustomed to grant their wives full liberty to contract a new engagement, or, at least, to live apart from their legal lords. An archbishop of Novgorod, Theodosius, bitterly complained of this practice. Up to the middle of the eighteenth century the Russian clergy dissolved the marriage bond very often for no other reason than that of incompatibility of temper, this incompatibility appearing in the dissolute life of either husband or wife.

The memory of those days is still preserved among the country folk, and we can explain the part taken by the customary Courts, in direct contradiction to the law, only by the influence on them of tradition. They take part in the making of certain contracts in which husbands and wives who no longer wish to live under the same roof, waive questions of interest, and agree to interfere no more with each other's existence.

The part which the community is called on to play in the contract and dissolution of marriage is strikingly manifested in certain peculiar ceremonies still in use at a Little Russian wedding. The tokens of the damsel's virginity are exhibited in much the same way as they were exhibited unto the elders of a Jewish city, as is described in the twenty-second chapter of Deuteronomy. The whole company then begin to shout loudly, congratulating the mother of the bride, and eulogising the maiden's virtue. In case the newly married wife is no longer a virgin, and her husband makes no statement as to his previous cohabitation with her, instead of praises and cheers, the most violent abuse is poured on the parents of the bride, and the most shameful songs are sung. They often go on to insulting acts, such as the following: spirits are offered in derision to the bride's mother in a glass with a hole in the bottom; the outside walls of the house are blackened with tar; a hole is made in the stove in order to show the stain which the hearth has suffered. Sometimes, also, one of the guests climbs up to the top of the house and begins to throw water down on all sides—a symbol of the liberality with which the new wife has distributed her favours to all those who asked for them. Very frequently, also, the parents of the bride are insulted by having yokes made of straw, previously besmeared with tar and dirt, placed by force on their necks.

The reciprocal rights and duties of husband and wife according to Russian customary law, and the position of children as regards their parents, are the next topics I intend to discuss in the present lecture.

The husband is acknowledged to be the master of the woman he has married. "The wife is in the power of her husband," so runs the common saying, and the fact of her complete subjection to his will is illustrated by certain symbolical acts performed at the time of the wedding. The bridegroom, while he is leading his bride to her future home, gives her from time to time light blows from a whip, saying at each stroke: "Forget the manners of thine own family, and learn those of mine." As soon as they have entered their bedroom, the husband says to his wife, "Take off my boots." The wife immediately obeys her husband's orders, and, taking them off, finds in one of them a whip, symbol of his authority over her person. This authority implies the right of the husband to control the behaviour of his wife, and to correct her every time he thinks fit, not only by words, but also by blows. The opinion which a Russian writer of the sixteenth century, the pope or priest Silvester (the author of *The Domostroy*), expressed as to the propriety of personal chastisement, and even as to its beneficial effects on the health, is still shared by the country people. In more than one popular song the wife is represented as bitterly complaining of the indifference of a husband who never on any occasion gives her a good beating. "I thrash those I love best," says a well-known Russian proverb. The customary Court seems to admit the use of such disciplinary proceedings by not interfering in the personal relations of husband and wife. "Never judge the quarrel of husband and wife," is a common saying, scrupulously observed by the village tribunals, which refuse to hear any complaint on the part of the aggrieved woman, at least so long as the punishment has not been of such a nature as to endanger life or limb. Where that is the case, the offender may be condemned to imprisonment, and the outraged victim allowed to retire for a time to the home of her parents. The customary law has, however, taken effectual measures for the protection of the wife's fortune. That husband and wife should each have entirely distinct property, with sole control over it, is still the leading principle at least in Great Russia. In the provinces which, like those of Little Russia, have been for centuries subject to the statute of Lithuania and the municipal law of Magdeburg, the system of a partial community of goods has prevailed. According to the customary law of Kiev, Poltava, and Chernigov, a widow has a right to the third part of the fortune left by her husband. In former times this third part was a sort of pledge for the security of the dowry of the wife.

A few words will suffice to give a general idea of the dependence in which the children are placed as regards their parents, and more especially their father. The patriarchal character of the Russian family plainly appears in the fact that no amount of bad treatment on the part of the parents justifies an appeal to the village tribunal, unless it involves danger to life or limb. In such cases, the nature of which makes it difficult to establish the facts before a Court of Law, the further maintenance of the child is generally committed to some near relative.

The complete dependence of the children upon their parents in respect to fortune is proved by the fact that neither son nor daughter can claim any portion of the family estate. The father can, as he pleases, give or refuse a dowry to his daughter. Should she marry against his wish no dowry is given, and she enters penniless into her husband's family. It equally depends upon the father's pleasure whether he shall transfer a portion of his property to a grown-up son, or maintain it intact in spite of his son's manifest wishes. An act of insubordination on the part of the son, as for instance, his marrying without permission, may become the occasion for his complete disinheritance by the father, at least so far as the father's fortune is concerned. I make this exception, inasmuch as, besides his share in the father's fortune, the son may be enabled to inherit from his mother's estate, or may possess property, the gift of some relative or friend. Such property must be scrupulously guarded by the father whose rights over it are only those of the natural guardian of his son's fortune.

Hitherto we have spoken of the Russian family as of a kind of natural society, created by marriage and continued by the birth of children; but side by side with this form of family organisation, differing only in detail from that of Western Europe, there exists in Russia a peculiar mode of family communism. In various parts of the country numerous persons, sometimes amounting to fifty and rarely to less than ten, are to be found united in a common household, living under the same roof and taking their meals at the same table. A family constituted after this fashion is known to English scholars under the name of "The Joint Family" or "House Community." Sir Henry Maine has made the notion of it generally familiar through his marvellous investigations in the early law of Ireland and the modern customs of Northern India. He has also correctly settled the question of its origin by appealing to natural increase and non-division as the real sources of its growth. He has even made an attempt to show that it was not limited to distinct peoples or races, but that, notwithstanding the immense distance which separates the Eastern or Hindoo branch of the Aryan race from the European branches, notwithstanding, also, the difference in the historical development which may be traced between its Celtic and Slavonic ramifications, joint households are as likely to be met with in the defiles of the Himalayas as in the plains of old Erin or of modern Servia. Taking advantage of the recent investigations made by Professor Bogisic in the customary law of the Southern Slavs, Sir Henry Maine has presented a lively picture of the interior organisation of the famous Servian "Zadrouga," which, as he shows, has more than one feature in common with the House Community of the Rajpoots. The barrier of language, of which he so often complains, prevented this master in the field of comparative jurisprudence from completing his studies of the patriarchal system of House Communities by investigating the Undivided Household of Great Russia. This Undivided Household has been recently the subject of numerous and serious inquiries on the part of Russian ethnographers; and the results of their investigations I desire now to lay before you.

First of all let me tell you that the undivided household of the Eastern Slavs is a very ancient institution. In the so-called Chronicle of Nestor, mention is made of the "gens" organisation of the Polians, a Slavonic tribe, dwelling as I have already said, on the banks of the Dnieper. The Polians are stated to live (I translate literally) "each ruling his own kindred or gens (rod svoi) and occupying distinct localities." This rather obscure text authorises the supposition that the Polians were divided into independent house-communities, each of which possessed its own piece of land. Another reference is made to these Undivided Households in one of the paragraphs of the Pravda of Jaroslav,* a sort of Mirror of Justice compiled in the middle of the eleventh century, by order of the Grand Duke Jaroslav, son of that Vladimir who introduced Christianity into Russia. The frequent occurrence of South Slavonic terms in this the oldest Russian code, such, for instance, as that of "bratouchada" (the son of the brother, the nephew) confirms the hypothesis first put forth, so far as I know, by the well-known professor of Russian history at Moscow, Mr. Kluchevsky, that the work of codification had been entrusted to some southern

* "The Pravda of Jaroslav," published by Kalachev, ss. 88, 89.

Slav. This is the more likely as owing to the recent introduction of Christianity and learning into Russia, there was a lack of well-educated natives, so that the Byzantine Church had frequently to have recourse to priests of South Slavonic origin, in order to propagate the Gospel and the elements of learning among their eastern and northern brethren. Old Russian being much more like the language into which the Holy Scriptures had been translated, and the Slavonic dialect of the translation being that of the Southern Slavs, priests of Bulgarian or Servian origin were the fittest persons in Russia to be employed in this work. The translation of Greek texts, the transcription and composition of Slavonic and Russian MSS., as also the first attempts at a written exposition of Russian customary law would equally fall into their hands. The share of a Southern Slav in the work of codification would explain the presence in the Pravda of Jaroslav of a term which has led to much comment. The word in question is *verv.* Various guesses had been made as to its meaning, when at last Professor Leontovitch had the good fortune to find it used in an old South Slavonic customary, the statute of Politza, and that in the sense of Undivided Household or House Community. The sense agrees with the context of the two paragraphs in which the word is used in the Pravda. In one of them mention is made of a case where the body of a man belonging to the "following" of the duke has been found within the limits of a *verv;* and the other says that in such a case the whole *verv* must pay in common a fine similar to that which was inflicted in England in such cases during the reigns of William the Conqueror and the early Plantagenets.

A "*verv,*" paying in common a sort of pecuniary composition for a crime supposed to have been committed by one of its members; a "*verv*" possessing its own proper limits, and therefore its own territorial possession, exactly corresponds to a house-community, in which several persons, living under the same roof and owning land in common, are jointly answerable for the crimes and misdemeanours committed within the limits of their possessions.

If from the eleventh and twelth centuries, during which the different versions of the Pravda were drawn up, we pass to the end of the fourteenth and the beginning of the fifteenth centuries, we find the same village community mentioned, as well in the North Western principalities of Russia—that of Pscov, for example, as in those of the South West which were ruled by the Statute of Lithuania. The name under which the members of these communities are known to the Russian law is that of "siabri." This term is employed both by the judicial charter of Pscov (1397–1467) and by the before-mentioned Statute of Lithuania (1529). This word *siabri* is also to be found among the Southern Slavs. The code of Servian laws, published by King Stefan Douschan in the year 1349, makes frequent use of it when speaking of the peasants.* The peasants of Servia, having always lived, and still living, in undivided households, the term meaning co-partners in the enjoyment of an undivided property, was very naturally applied to them and it is this meaning that the word still keeps in the judicial charter of Pscov, and also in the Statute of Lithuania. The latter was the chief source of the customary law of Little Russia, and the term "siabri" and the institution it calls to mind, are often mentioned in the Little Russian documents of the last three centuries. A recent survey of these sources, made by Professor Louchitzky, has quite settled the question of the existence of House Communities even in those provinces of Little Russia where in our time division of property most prevails. Here as elsewhere individualism seems to have been preceded by a sort of family communism like that of India, Ireland and the South Slavonian principalities.

The term *siabri* is not the only one used by Old Russian writers to designate the members of such a household. They are often spoken of in the financial surveys of the sixteenth and seventeenth centuries under the characteristic name of hearth, *pechische.* The so-called *piszoviia knigi*, a kind of survey very like the poll-tax rolls still preserved in the Record Office, speak of the hearth as the unit of taxation.

* This word appears, for instance, in the following sentences: "No political assembly of the 'siabri' ought to exist." "If any one convenes it, let him lose his ears."

The *pechische* of the fifteenth and sixteenth centuries corresponds to the *feu* of Burgundy and is even known by that name in some of the northern provinces of Russia. The private charters, which are still preserved by more than one family in the Government of Archangel, some of which were drawn up in the sixteenth and seventeenth centuries, when speaking of the house community always make use of the term *ognische*, a word which means the hearth-fire, thus showing that what constituted the tie between members of the same household was their cooking food at the same hearth.

Thus far we have shown the high antiquity of the institution which we are engaged in examining. Let us now proceed to the study of its characteristic features.

All over Russia, but particularly within the boundaries of the old Muscovite empire, communities of persons belonging to the same kindred and living under the same roof are still in existence. The number of persons belonging to these communities varies from ten, or even less, to fifty and upwards. In the Government of Koursk a community composed of about sixty persons has recently been noticed by Professor Samokvasov. But such cases are rare, and the number of persons living in common does not, as a rule, exceed twenty or thirty. Among them we find the grandfather and grandmother, the father and mother, sons and daughters, grandsons and granddaughters, brothers and sisters, nephews and nieces, with such other persons as may be united to them by ties of marriage, as daughters-in-law in right of their husbands, and sons-in-law in right of their wives. Persons incorporated into the family, working for the common good, and having shares in the family profits are often mentioned by writers on Russian folk-lore. Besides these others may perchance have become members, as for instance persons adopted into it, or the children of a widow contracting a new marriage with a member of the community, who, on account of her unwillingness to be separated from them, come to live with her under the roof of her new husband.

From this we see how various may have been the origin of those who were members of the Undivided Family. Blood-relationship, in the proper sense of the word, is not always required, it suffices that the members be *considered* as relatives; adoption takes the place of actual descent, and the fact of sharing the daily work very often gives a stranger the rights of a relative.

Undivided households are, as a rule, governed by the oldest members of the community, but in case of prolonged illness or want of mental power the oldest member may be superseded by another, sometimes elected by the whole community. The name given to the house-elder is *bolschack*, which means the greatest in power. His authority and functions perfectly correspond to those belonging, in a Servian *zadruga*, to the so-called "domachin." Like the domachin, he is assisted in the difficult task of governing the female part of the house community by some aged woman, known by the name of "bolschoucha" (the greatest woman), who is not always his wife.

It would be a gross error to look upon the house-elder of a Russian undivided family as holding the same position as the Roman paterfamilias. The house-elder has neither the authority nor the amount of independence enjoyed by the paterfamilias in the administration of the family fortune. The Russian house-elder, like the Servian domachin, is but *primus inter pares*. All the grown-up members of the community constitute a sort of family council, whose advice must be regularly asked in matters of importance. The domachin has no right to dispose of the family possessions without the unanimous consent of all the persons for whom he acts. When I say *all*, I mean of course only the grown-up members, women as well as men. The women's opinion, though of less importance than the men's, is not to be disregarded, the more so on account of the influence which they exercise on their husbands.

The functions of the house-elder are of very various kinds. We must mention first of all his exclusive right to represent the community before the executive and judicial authorities of the village and district (selo i volost). It is he who regularly appears in the courts, either to answer the complaints against the community, or to insist on the recognition of rights which have been violated. It is to him also that the Government officials address their demand for the speedy payment of the taxes. It is his duty to attend to the execution of the law concerning military service, and to the carrying out of the different orders issued by the local and provincial authorities.

As to the duties which the domachin has to perform in connection with the interior administration of the household, they are of two different kinds: they concern either the persons who compose the house community, or the undivided property owned by them. All disputes arising between co-partners are settled by the house-elder, who is regularly assisted in such cases by the family council. His interference in the relations between husband and wife, between parents and children, sometimes exerts a highly beneficial influence, in so far as it prevents cases of gross abuse in the exercise of marital and paternal power; but it often happens on the other hand that disputes between married couples are embittered by the partiality of the house-elder for one or other party. On more than one occasion husbands have been known to inflict severe punishment on their wives because they were ordered to do so by the head of the community; instances, too, are very frequent in which the wife, encouraged by the support of the house-elder, disregards the rights of her husband, and lives in almost open adultery with the person whose chief duty ought to consist in the maintenance of a high moral standard amongst the persons over whom he exercises authority.

The house-elder has also, if not a casting vote, at least a consultative voice in such matters as the choice of a wife, or the giving of a daughter in marriage. As the amount of the dowry is always fixed by the family council, presided over by its chief, his decision very often settles the question as to the acceptance or refusal of the offer of marriage. It is also the duty of the house-elder to find occupation for the unemployed members of the household. If the community is too large to allow of all its members being employed in agricultural labour, the family finds it advantageous to permit a certain number of its members to seek their fortunes abroad, either in private service or as small traders or pedlars, travelling about the country with packs on their backs. Such petty hawkers, very numerous in our Eastern provinces, are known in Russia under the various names of "ofeni," "chodebocschiki," "korobhniki," and "prosoli." They render a real service to the country population, which, at least in places far distant from railways and markets, would without them have no means of procuring the most simple necessaries of life.

Young orphans find in the person of the house-elder their legal guardian; their moral and mental education depends solely on him; it is he who sends them to school, finds employment for them in the fields, or apprentices them to the different village artisans to learn a trade by which to earn a future livelihood.

As the administration of the family fortune, as I have already said, falls on the house-elder, he makes all arrangements that are needful to secure that every kind of agricultural labour shall be properly done, assigning to each his daily share in the ploughing, harrowing, and sowing of the fields. thrashing of the corn, and such like occupations. If the number of hands of which the family can dispose is not sufficient to answer all its requirements, he hires others to help them. When the time comes for the exchange of harvest produce for such articles as the peasants may need, it is again the business of the house-elder to sign contracts of sale or exchange. Those under his charge have in such cases the right to control actions and to demand a full account of all the moneys received or paid by him.

This control is particularly useful on those somewhat rare occasions when, in consequence of a series of bad harvests, the family is obliged to dispose of a part of its estate. On such occasions the whole family has a voice in the selection of the purchases. Their unanimous consent, plainly expressed in the act of sale, is necessary in order to render it legal.

The resources by which the family provides for all its requirements are of different kinds: some are derived from the lands it owns, others from the private earnings of its members. Widely separated though some of its members may be from the family, the travelling pedlar, the labourer who has hired himself out on some distant farm, the soldier and sailor fighting in some foreign country or sailing to some distant land, nevertheless they all look upon it a duty to allow their family to share in their earnings. On its part the House Community does not object to maintain the wife and children of an absent member, or to pay the amount of his yearly taxes. The communistic character of the great Russian family is shown by the ease with which the household gets its members who are temporarily separated from it to pay over to it the gains which they make. These, as a rule, make no claim to keep their earnings for themselves. The *peculium castrense* and *quasi castrense,* formerly known to the ancient Romans, appear still to exist among the members of the Russian house communities of the present day. If a movement in favour of the establishment of private property can be detected it is only in the private earnings made by the women and girls in their leisure hours. These earnings accumulated hour by hour and day by day form, as a rule, the principal part of the future dowry, the father and mother making but a small addition to the sum got together by the industry and thrift of a maiden who for many years has been preparing for her marriage. The Undivided Household of Great Russia may in this respect be compared to the house community of India, for it also secures to an unmarried woman the right of providing a *peculium* apart, a sort of independent fortune, the so-called "stridhana," by the accumulation of the small savings she regularly makes by needlework.

Now that I have traced, though only in its general outlines, that peculiar institution known in Russia under the rather vague term of "The Great Family," let me call your attention to the advantages and disadvantages which this institution presents. Its great merit certainly consists in the fact that it develops to a far larger extent than the small families of our days the feeling of mutual dependence and joint relationship without which no system of social reform can have any chance of success. Possessing as they do no other but common property and having an equal share in all the material enjoyments of fortune, the members of these communistic bodies escape from the disheartening influence of economic competition.

The conditions of this existence necessarily develop in them all the consciousness of mutual responsibility, and the conviction that without reliance on one another they cannot overcome the dangers and difficulties of life. It would be a study of high psychological interest to analyse the character of a people which had grown up under such conditions, and to show how far the inborn selfish instincts of man have been moderated by the softening influence of a state of society which, to a certain extent, does away with the necessity for an uninterrupted struggle for life. The Russian novelists, conscious of what might properly be expected of them, have more than once tried to give a picture of the Russian "moujik" who is so unlike the French "paysan," that petty owner of a small piece of land jealously watched and guarded from the encroachments of his neighbour and from those of the State.

The life-like characters drawn by our great author, Tourgenieff, in his vivid "Sketches of a Sportsman" are, I believe, the best illustrations that have ever been given of the thoughts and feelings of our people —a people who, though rough and rude, yet enjoy the great blessing of being unconscious of the need of securing their individual happiness by a constant struggle and by the pursuit of egotistic ends. The reliance shown by the Russian peasant on the community, his conviction that the *mir* is always just and reasonable, and that truth is nowhere to be found but in the unanimous opinion of the people have certainly developed estimable qualities and have helped to make the Russian *moujik* a communist. That this is really the case, and that his character has been modified by the system of the Great Family, is proved by the fact that wherever a division of the common property had taken place, wherever the peasant has been reduced by his own will to depend entirely on his personal industry for his success in life, he has become the pushing, unscrupulous man whom the American novelist has rendered so familiar to us. Two great Russian writers, Mr. Ouspensky and Mr.

Slatovraczky, both equally unknown to the English public although their popularity amongst my countrymen almost equals that of Tourgenieff or Tolstoi, have recently published two widely different accounts of the social and psychological condition of our peasants. Mr. Ouspensky has spoken of the peasant as a creature whose ethics almost entirely depend upon the regular performance of agricultural labour. As long as he remains a proprietor his morals are sound, but let him once lose the piece of land which he has made fruitful by the sweat of his brow he is sure to fall into debauchery and vice. Mr. Slatovraczky has depicted him as a kind of unselfish philosopher, who thinks that the products of the earth are the common inheritance of all men, and that the chief duty of a Christian is to help his neighbour, sometimes even at his own expense.

Now, what may seem hardly credible is that both authors have been applauded by the same public—applauded, moreover, because both were equally correct in their statements. The key to the mystery is to be found in the fact that it is a different life which is pictured by each—the first having chosen his hero from among the members of a broken-up house community; the second among those still living in common. Our thoughts and feelings being directly influenced by our social conditions, Mr. Ouspensky's hero presents to us all the features of a hard worker, pursuing no other object than his own interests and welfare, whilst Mr. Slatovraczky's hero appears to be "a person living not after the word of man but after the word of God," caring for his fellow-creatures almost as much as for himself.*

There is exaggeration in the way in which both authors represent the modern Russian *moujik;* for the sense of proportion which was so highly valued by the ancients is not always possessed by my countrymen; but even taking into account this partiality for certain social forms and institutions, I believe they have rendered us a real service by pointing out the intimate correspondence that exists between the moral character of our peasantry and their ancient mode of life.

I must, nevertheless, confess that morality, that at least which is concerned with the relations between the sexes, has not much to gain from the close packing under the same roof of persons differing in sex and age. I leave to Mr. Anatole Leroy Beaulieu the task of instructing you on this subject: "Chez un peuple pauvre et chez des hommes grossiers," says this acute French observer, "tout n'est point profit et vertu sous le régime patriarcal. On sait combien de maux de toutes sortes dérivent dans les grandes villes d'occident, de l'étroitesse des logements et de l'entassement des individus. Les inconvenients ne sont pas moindres en Russie. Quand une étroite izba (chaumière) réunit plusieurs générations et plus-

* The two novels to which I allude are, "The Power of Land," by Ouspensky, and "The Solid Base" (Oustoi), by Slatovraczky. Both novels were published in Moscow.

ieurs ménages, que durant les longues nuits d'un long hiver les pères et les enfants, les frères et leurs femmes couchent pêle-mêle autour du large poêle, il en résulte une sorte de promiscuité aussi malsaine pour l'âme que pour le corps. Chez le moujik, alors même que les enfants mariés habitaient plusieurs izbas disposées autour de la même cour, l'autocratie domestique était un danger pour l'intégrité et la chasteté de la famille. De même que le propriétaire noble sur les serves de ses domaines, le chef de maison s'arrogeait parfois une sorte de droit du seigneur sur les femmes soumises à son autorité. Le chef, désigné du surnom le Vieux, qui, grâce à la précocité des marriages, avait souvent à peine quarante ans, prélevait sur ses belles filles un tribut que la jeunesse ou la dépendance de ses fils leur défendait de lui contester. Il n'était point rare de voir ainsi le foyer domestique souillié par l'autorité qui en devait maintenir la pureté.*

It may also certainly be questioned how far the loss of a spirit of personal enterprise, and the removal of a strong feeling of self-reliance ought to be considered beneficial. I have no doubt that if modern Russia produces on the minds of foreign observers an impression as of a land of paupers, the reason of it, or at least one of the reasons, is to be found in the prevalence of these old communistic institutions. We must not forget that it is the principle of self-

* "L'Empire des Tzars et les Russes," p. 488.

help that has created the material growth of England and of the United States of America. But in entering on these discussions I trench on very uncertain ground. The relative advantages and disadvantages of individualism and of communism have furnished matter for warm controversy from the time of Plato down to the time of Ruskin and of Spencer, and we need not discuss them here. I think it better to state that the Russian peasant, at least in our time, is not insensible to the advantages of individualism, as is well shown by the fact that between two and three million divisions of House Communities have been effected since the day when the liberated serf obtained the right to make them. If divisions of family property were rare before 1861, the year of the abolition of serfdom, the reason lies in the fact that the manorial lords and the State were alike interested in the preservation of the system of Undivided Households. The natural responsibility of the members for the payment of taxes and for the execution of those various kinds of agricultural labour which serfs were bound to perform on the lands of the manor, were advantages far too precious to be easily abandoned. It was, and it still is, for the interests of the national treasury that these divisions should not take place. It is for this reason that the Government, concealing its real designs under a show of good-will towards an old and venerable institution, has recently taken measures to prevent further divisions. It is no longer with the majority that the decision is to rest in questions of this kind, but with the chief of the household, a person who is, of course, as a rule, interested in the maintenance of non-division.

The reasons which are brought forward by the peasants to justify their breaking up of Undivided Households are generally the following: Non-division, they say, causes the able and laborious to work for the idle and incapable. It is unjust to force an unmarried person to divide his savings with a relative enjoying the pleasures of married life and a numerous progeny, who, on account of their youth, are not yet able to earn anything by the work of their hands. They also affirm that, as the dwelling-place is too small to accommodate a large family, they are forced to divide in order to live with decency.

It is also often said that disputes among the women are the direct cause of separation, while, again, some peasants frankly avow that they insist on leaving their communistic mode of life in order to have their own homes and to be their own masters.* If the objections just mentioned are not those of individualism, I do not know what individualism is.

It is in the most fertile regions of Russia—in Little Russia and New Russia—that divisions have

* Compare what M. Dobrotvorsky says about the family in the Government of Vladimir (*Juridical Journal*, Moscow, 1889, vol. ii. p. 283).

been most numerous. In these parts small families are already the general rule, as the black soil of those districts is rich enough to pay the taxes that are levied, and the peasant is not alarmed by the prospect of being deprived of the aid of his relatives. The spirit of independence of the Cossacks, which all those who are acquainted with them readily acknowledge, explains to a great extent the reason why the undivided household is dying out in the southern and south-western parts of Russia.

The northern provinces will certainly sooner or later follow the same path, and the patriarchal house community will disappear in Russia, just as it has disappeared in France, Italy, and Spain, and as it is disappearing in our days in Servia and Croatia. For we must not think that this system was altogether unknown to the people of Western Europe. Not only in Ireland, where its previous existence had been recognised by Sir Henry Maine, but also among the German and Latin races, the undivided household was, a few centuries ago, a still living institution. Guy Coquille, a legal writer of the sixteenth century, speaks of them in the province of Nivernais, and they have recently been discovered in the old charters of Berry. The "consorteria" of mediæval Tuscany, the "genealogiæ" of the old Alemannic law, and the still existing "Companias" of Spanish Galicia, are but different names to designate the Undivided Household. If these have disappeared, or are likely to disappear, in the near future, it is because they have been forced to yield to the requirements of individualism. I see no reason why the same thing should not happen in Russia.

# LECTURE III.

## THE PAST AND PRESENT OF THE RUSSIAN VILLAGE COMMUNITY.

Few questions of history are debated in our days as that of the origin of village communities. French, English, and German scholars, to say nothing of Russians and Americans, have published whole volumes in order to prove either the existence or non-existence of village communities in that period of evolution which is generally known as patriarchal.

The acute German observer, Baron Haxthausen, who was the first to describe to European readers the social and economic character of the Russian *mir*, was probably quite unconscious of the literary movement to which he was to give rise by his two or three sentences about the antiquity of the Russian agrarian community, and its likeness to the social and economic institutions of the Southern and Western Slavs. A few years after the publication of Baron Haxthausen's work, a Moscovite professor, Mr. Chicherin, in two articles which at once produced a great sensation, strongly protested against the opinion that Russian village communities were the direct descendants of those undivided households which so commonly form part of the historical past of most Aryan nations. The Slavophils and their leader Chomiakov maintained that they were the spontaneous growth of Russia. Chicherin believed they had a twofold origin—that they were partly the creation of a Government anxious to secure an easy method of collecting one of the taxes which was very like the old French capitation tax, and partly due to the landed aristocracy, which could find no better means than an equal and periodical redistribution of the land, for attaching to the soil those classes of the people who were reduced to the condition of serfdom. This extraordinary assertion immediately met with a systematic denial on the part of Mr. Beliaiev, the well-known Professor of Legal History, who was one of the colleagues of Mr. Chicherin, and whose extensive researches in the legal history of Russia gave his opinion great weight. This did not, however, prevent M. Fustel de Coulanges from reproducing the theory just as if it had not already been refuted. But the inventors of theories, of whom Fustel de Coulanges was certainly one of the greatest, too often follow the method described in the well-known French saying: "Je prends mon bien où je le trouve." Seeing that a denial of the antiquity of the Russian village communities supported his theory of the general prevalence of private property even in the earliest times, he thought himself at liberty to disregard all later investigations, and to endorse an opinion which had already been refuted.

The study of the origin and growth of Russian village communities has never been discontinued in my country since the time when the work of Haxthausen first drew the attention of our economists and historians to this peculiar institution. A crowd of young students have rendered familiar, even to the general public, the notion that they were the spontaneous result of our social development; that the Government, by interfering in their internal constitution, has only succeeded in obscuring their national character; that mutual responsibility in matters of taxation was foreign to their original organisation; and that there is ample foundation for the statement that their members, from being, as they were at first, free possessors of the soil, became the serfs of the Czar, the nobles, or the clergy.

The extraordinary increase of historical research in Russia, and especially of investigations into the social and economical development of the country, which took place during the reign of Alexander II., certainly contributed largely to induce German scholars, with the illustrious Maurer at their head, to review the current opinions concerning the social condition of the Germans in the Middle Ages. It led Maurer to elaborate his magnificent theory of the Mark, Manor, and Village Constitution (Mark, Hof und Dorf Verfassung).

Sir Henry Maine made the system of village communities familiar to English students, and had, moreover, the great merit of showing that, far from being a peculiar feature of the social organisation of the Germans and Slavs, they were to be found amongst the majority of Aryan nations, in the plains of the Punjab and the interior of the North-West Provinces of India, and among the green pastures of Erin. The almost universal admiration which his essay on Village Communities in the East and West has elicited, rests on no other ground than that of its having first brought to light the truth which is now all but established, that village communities represent a distinct period in the social development of mankind, a period which ought to be placed between the patriarchal and the feudal periods, and that, therefore, all endeavours to explain their existence among this or that people by the peculiarities of national character ought to be henceforth declared useless and worthless.

This idea, confirmed, as it is, by a general survey of the survivals left by the system of village communities among the Celtic, German, and Latin nations, a survey with which M. de Laveleye has inseparably connected his name, has literally revolutionised the historical researches of more than one country of Europe, and especially those of my own. The impression produced by the two writers just mentioned is still so strong that Russian scholars, instead of subscribing to the recent ingenious hypothesis of Mr.

Seebohm as to the servile origin of village communities in England, have themselves set to work to examine the rich materials which the Bodleian Library and the Record Office present as to the history of land-ownership in England. In saying this I have particularly in view the deep and accurate studies of my former colleague Professor Vinogradov on the agrarian constitution of mediæval England, of which a few years ago I gave a short account in the *Law Quarterly Review*. Others have made similar inquiries into the economic history of mediæval Germany, and their studies have induced some French authors. and among them M. Dareste, warmly to oppose the original but one-sided theory of Fustel de Coulanges.

Before passing to the direct study of the development of the Russian village community, I must recognise the fact that the long and sometimes violent struggle of the early Slavophils on behalf of the spontaneous origin of the *mir*, has been productive of the best results to the study of agrarian communism in Russia.

A comparison between the modern constitution of the *mir* and that described in old charters proves the widely different character of the two, while the differences between them support the theory of a natural evolution of the community, an evolution not yet completed in more than one part of the Empire. The difference which we trace between the past and the present of the Russian commune, are the same which we see existing between the various modern forms of it in our own day. The study, therefore, of these forms and of their natural transformation may be of great help towards understanding the true origin and growth of the system. The opportunity—I may even say the necessity—of such a study is the more apparent on account of the lack of mediæval documents concerning the early constitution of the *mir*. Our sources of information are limited indeed; for several centuries, down to the end of the fifteenth, they are almost entirely wanting, and they only begin to be at all abundant during the last three hundred years. It is only, therefore, by a survey of the modern evolution of village ownership in some remote parts of Russia that we can get an idea of the various transformations which the commune has had to undergo before it reached its present condition.

The vastness of the area and the fact that certain parts of Russia remained for centuries unpeopled, partly on account of their physical condition, partly owing to their insecurity, due, as it was, to the periodical invasions of the Tartars, explain, to a great extent, why the character of the commune varies so much throughout the land. Its growth has been stopped in one place at an early stage, in another place at a later stage, of its development. We can trace these stages in some cases by charters and by legal and judicial documents, in others by the transformation of the commune into higher and more elaborate forms. It is only by the study of these documents and these forms that the Russian historian can hope to be able to describe the gradual development of the agrarian communism of his country. We will now consider the chief results which the application of this method has produced.

In the last lecture it was shown that the earliest mode of land tenure in Russia was the holding it in an undivided state by the members of a house community. This kind of a family communism is mentioned in the Pravda of Jaroslav at the end of the eleventh century, and continued to exist in the north and south of the country down to the seventeenth and eighteenth centuries. The chief characteristic of this holding consisted in the fact that, though the land remained undivided and lay open as it had done for centuries before, every member of the household, nevertheless, was the possessor of a share in the various fields belonging to the family. These shares were not equal, but varied according to rights of inheritance appertaining to each of the holders. Should the brothers and nephews decide on living separately, they would abandon the old system of using in common the produce of the early harvest, and divide the area of the arable land in unequal shares, proportioned to the rights of inheritance possessed by each member of the household. The extent of the shares was not fixed. The soil varied in fertility, and all the shareholders alike appreciated the advantages of vicinity; each partner, therefore, received the right to enjoy a certain portion in each of the fields possessed by the village. These portions were not strictly defined, but, as a rule, represented the half, third, fourth, eighth, and so on, of the field according to the heritage which was acknowledged to belong to each partner.

Let us suppose the case of one commune, the family consisting of three brothers living and two nephews, the sons of a fourth brother deceased. The share of each of the brothers would be one-fourth part of each of the different fields in the village, whilst that of the nephews would not exceed an eighth. Each partner having a right to sell his ideal portion, or a part of it, to a stranger, as well as to a relative, the village would soon become occupied by neighbours owning the most unequal portions in field. These neighbours would maintain the obligations which common possession is apt to establish; the meadows for the greater part of the time would be kept undivided, subject here and there to a yearly distribution according to the wants of each homestead; but these wants being as a rule the same, the custom would prevail of dividing them into equal parts for the purpose of mowing.

The pasture and forest land would also remain subject to a community of ownership, and would sometimes belong to several neighbouring villages, which in that case would constitute a larger area, similar to the German "mark," and known under the name of "volost." Each of the inhabitants of the "volost" would be allowed an unlimited use of the undivided area, it being too extensive to be easily exhausted. It would, however, be an error to suppose that this general and unlimited enjoyment of the undivided mark was but the result of that freedom which all possessed as to unoccupied ground (the *res nullius*), for a person who was not an inhabitant of the village or villages constituting the mark or "volost," would have no right to enjoy its pastures and forest lands. That this was the case is proved by the fact that no one might dig a piece of ground belonging to the forest unless the digging were authorised by the whole community of shareholders. Such a right of prohibition could not have been enjoyed unless the community was the owner of the "mark."

The natural evolution of agrarian communism did not go further than this in the northern parts of Russia. It went further, however, in the south—in those vast and fertile steppes which lie on the eastern and western banks of Dnieper, and which for centuries constituted a part of Poland. The recent researches of Professor Louchizky have brought to light the following facts, which were quite unknown and some of which were directly contradicted by former historians. Undivided households and their immediate successors, villages, composed of sharers in the same ground, were in the beginning well known on the eastern bank of the Dnieper. The undivided "mark," on which every homestead had the right to take fuel and to pasture its cattle, is known in this region under the name of lands belonging to the "gromada," or commune. They are sometimes called also common or village lands. The colonists who, during the sixteenth and seventeenth centuries, crossed the river in order to occupy the free steppes in the modern Government of Tchernigov, migrated in companies, organised on the model of undivided or partly divided households. These companies were called "skladchina," from the verb "skladivat," which means to put something in common. The area on which the colonisation took place was so boundless that each homestead was allowed to sow yearly as much ground as it was able to till. When the harvest was once reaped the land was abandoned, and a new piece occupied for agricultural purposes. You can easily see that this was a proceeding similar to that of the ancient Germans, of which Tacitus says:—"Arva per annos mutant et superest ager."

I need not tell you that as long as the population was small enough to allow of a yearly change of soil for cultivation, redistribution was never thought of; no mention is ever made of the run-rig system which characterises the modern village community. But as it is impossible that shares should be equal without recourse to some such method, we must not look for equality under the conditions just stated. Even in the eighteenth century, when the growth of population had diminished the area of arable land, periodical redistribution remained unknown. If some amount of equality was, nevertheless, secured, it was due to the control which the commune began to exert over its members. Private appropriation of soil was no longer allowed, except on the condition of its being made at certain fixed periods, and under the supervision of the authorities. Twice a year, in autumn and in spring, the whole commune, with its cattle and its agricultural implements, went out into the open field. At the command of the village-elder, the head of each homestead proceeded to trace with his own plough the limits of the ground he intended to sow, and no one was allowed to extend his cultivation beyond the limits thus settled. By-and-by the right of retaining these private parcels of ground was extended to a period of three years, at the end of which they returned to the commune, and a new appropriation of the arable area was ordered to be made.

Hitherto I have spoken of the mode in which land was enjoyed so far as it applied to arable land alone. Let us now say a word about the meadows, forest land, and pastures. The first were owned on conditions similar to those first mentioned. At the end of May a day was fixed when all the villagers were assembled for the hay harvest. Each householder marked with a scythe the limits of the meadow he intended to mow. It was the duty of the village-elders to see that these limits were strictly observed. Forests and pastures were so abundant that no measuring was needed to regulate their use. Non-division and common enjoyment remained the general rule, several villages very often possessing equal rights to take fuel and to pasture cattle in the same forests and wastes.

Whilst this was the state of things on the banks of the Dnieper, a similar evolution took place on those of the Don. An area, even larger than that of the south-western steppes in the middle of the sixteenth century, awaited the arrival of those Great Russian colonists, who founded the so-called Territory of the Don-Cossacks. For a while the ground was declared to be the common property of the whole community, and each family was allowed to sow and mow wherever it liked, but by-and-by large villages called "stanitza" were formed, and the first division of the ground took place. Each village received its own area of arable and meadow ground; pasture and waste land remained the common property of the whole people, or, as it was said, of the whole "army."

The unlimited right of private homesteads to appropriate as much soil as each required was scrupulously maintained by these stanitzas, a fact which in the end produced great inequality in the distribution of the land. This inequality was established in favour of a minority of families out of which the elders of the people were regularly chosen; but as those who were possessed of but small parcels of land formed the majority, various economic arrangements were regularly made at the village folkmotes where this majority was all powerful; redistributions of land in order to equalise the shares were very often prescribed and the system of run-rig tenure made its first appearance. This took place almost in our own time, some few stanitzas continuing even now to maintain their ancient privilege of private appropriation.

I might continue my survey of the beginnings of the modern system of village communities by a description of the economic arrangements still in use among the Cossacks of the Terek or of the Oural, but if I did so, I should only have to repeat the same facts, and that in order to deduce the following conclusions. That the modern system of periodical redistribution of land in equal shares was quite unknown when colonisation first began, but that this did not prevent a peculiar kind of agrarian communism, the foundations of which are to be traced in the internal constitution of the undivided household; and that this form of social existence was known to Russia at the beginning of her history, and was diffused all over her empire, as may be seen from the frequent occurrence in mediæval documents of terms like "the hearth," "the fire" (pechische, ognische).

All the districts we have passed in review had one thing in common; serfdom was almost unknown to them. The peasants of Archangel for instance were always named "svoiezemzi," which means independent possessors of the soil. Social distinctions remained almost unknown to the Little Russians down to the end of the eighteenth century when Catherine the Second introduced amongst them the notions of a feudal nobility and serfdom. The Cossacks of the Don remained free up to the time of Nicholas. I am, therefore, right in saying that agrarian communism is not the direct result of serfdom, since it has been shown to exist in regions where serfdom was unknown.

A careful study of old Russian documents does not add much to the strength of this argument. The illiterate peasants could not consign to writing the economic arrangements they entered into, and in this fact lies the true reason why, out of the various categories into which the Russian peasantry was divided during the middle ages, none is less familiar to us than the free villager, the occupier of the so-called "black hundreds" (chernia sotni). The commune was completely independent in matters of internal concern, there was no need for the government or for judicial charters to meddle in its system of land tenure. What information we can gather from them of the external organisation of the *volost* or commune proves however the prevalence of a communistic and democratic mode of existence. The assembly of the people, the folkmote, called in the South Western provinces of Russia the "veche," more often "the copa," was formed of all the house-elders of a volost. It possessed the right of making local bye-laws; of choosing the elders of the commune or "starostas"; of distributing among its members the direct taxes which the government imposed on agriculture and on the different industries of the nation (sochi i promisli). Persons were also chosen by the commune to assist the judges in the exercise of their duties, playing on this occasion the part reserved in mediæval Germany to the so-called Schöffen and in old Sweden to the "nemd."*

As to the relation in which the volost stood to the ground that it occupied, this subject is partly illustrated by the following facts.

We possess a small number of private charters and judicial records, belonging to the fifteenth and the sixteenth centuries, from which we may see, that the true owner of the soil was partly the village and partly the "volost," or association of villagers. To give you an instance of what I am saying, I will cite the precise text of some of these charters.

In 1555 a lawsuit began between a squire (votchinnik) called Nefediev and the peasants of eighteen villages all belonging to the volost of Almesch. The question which the judges had to decide, was whether

* "See Ivanischev, "On the Old Village Communities in South-Western Russia" (Works, page 231); Gorchacov, "The Landed Property of the Metropolitans, Patriarchs, and Holy Synod," p. 210; Sergievich, "Lectures and Inquiries into the History of Russian Law," p. 668.

some pastures belonged to the volost or to the squire. Witnesses named by each party from among the oldest inhabitants of the locality declared that the peasants were the real possessors of the ground in dispute, and that their ownership went back to a period beyond the memory of man, and the judge decided that the claims of the squire were null and void.

In the case just mentioned we find ourselves in presence of a sort of undivided mark, composed, like that of Germany, of a certain number of villages possessing lands in common. These lands are pastures. Other charters of the same period show us cases in which the undivided area of the mark or volost was composed of forest ground. Expressions like the following are frequent in the documents just mentioned: "The forest belongs to the commune (selo) and the villages in common (vopsche), or "this" piece of forest ground has been given to me by the volost (the mark), the elder, and the peasants."

No one had the right to clear the forest or reclaim the waste land lying within the limits of a volost, unless authorised to do so by the elders and the assembly of peasants. This fact appears clearly in the following instance: In 1524, three persons found some salt wells on the shores of Dvina in the midst of a dark forest. They addressed a petition to the Government asking to be recognised as the legal possessors of the place, and they supported their demand by the following argument: "Not one of the surrounding marks or volosts has any appurtenances in the place." Had it been otherwise, had the wells been situated on the appurtenances of a volost, no private person could have made the demand just mentioned. The marks or volosts jealously watched over the integrity of their boundaries, and that from the earliest times. In the "Lives of the Saints," those early monuments of our written literature, complaint is sometimes made of peasants doing their best to get rid of a hermit, established in a neighbouring forest, "because," says the hagiographer, "they feared he would assign to some monastery a part of the ground they owned."*

The charters give, as I have already said, very little information about the internal arrangements of the volost and village; all we know is that the settlements were very far from resembling those large assemblages of people which are known in our days under the name of "slobodi." As a rule the "derevnia" or village contained few hearths, and the villages were scattered over the whole area of the volost. The wastes and forests were used in common, while the meadows and arable fields became the object of private appropriation. No equality of shares seem to have existed, the charters constantly mentioning the "best men," "the men of wealth," (jitii liudi) side by side with the "smaller men" (molodschii). Some few seem to have had even no

* See "The Life of Dimitry Prilouzky."

part at all in the possessions of the soil, being known under the name of podsousedi or podsousedki, which means living under the authority of a neighbour or villager (sosed). These persons were regularly employed as agricultural labourers. Some few, the so-called "bobili," were possessed of small parcels of land, resembling in that the *cottarii* of Domesday Book. The agricultural area owned by each homestead was known by the name of "jrebii," which means a lot, and the sense which men of the thirteenth and fourteenth centuries attached to this term is revealed to us by an old Russian translation of some parts of the Byzantine codes, the Prochiron and the Eclogue. This translation in certain points appears to be a kind of adaptation of Greek legislation to the conditions of the Russian people. One of the paragraphs of these so-called "Books of the Law" (Zakonnii Knigi, chap. xii.) contains the following sentence: "If a division of land shall take place by which some person shall injure the interest of others in their plots (jrebii) the division must not be maintained."*

The jrebii being a plot of land enjoyed by a single household out of the agricultural area of the mark, a plot which need not necessarily be equal to those of the neighbours, we are right in saying that the village community of the free peasants of Muscovy was like that of the Cossacks of the Dnieper. This likeness is to a certain extent obscured

* Pavlov, "Knigi Zakonnii," sec. 10, p. 44.

by the financial arrangements which the Muscovite volost entered into in order to secure the yearly payment of the land tax, these arrangements, as well as the tax itself, being quite unknown to Little Russian communes.

The Muscovite administration formerly empowered the volosts to distribute the taxes imposed on the villages, according to the quantity of cultivated land together with the commons thereto annexed, possessed by them. The sum to be paid by the inhabitants of each subdivision of the mark was then divided among the various households according to the extent of their possessions. The unit of taxation was the land of a plough. I mean the amount of land which one plough, working the whole day, could turn up. This unit was known by the name of "socha." Some homesteads owned two, three, or more of these, but there were others who held only a portion of this unit, just as in mediæval England there were households owning entire virgates, or the half or third part of a virgate, and in Germany there were holders of "mansi pleni et mansi dimidii," "ganze und halbe Hufen." As serfdom was unknown and no mutual responsibility in matters of taxation bound the peasant to the soil he occupied, undivided households very often quitted their dwellings in order to settle in some neighbouring country, on lands still free of occupation, or on those liberally accorded to new-comers by their private owners, on condition of a small payment.

The abandoned ground returned each time to the volost, which always took measures to find some new occupier who might relieve the mark from the increase of taxation produced by the departure of the previous occupier. Instances of such new occupation are regularly reported in the following terms: "All the peasants of the volost have allowed such and such persons to settle on the lots (jrebii) left free by the departure of such and such persons. The *mir* (this word means the whole community of shareholders) has conceded this lot to——" (here follows the name). The shares of each particular household having no distinct limits, we are induced to think that the possession of a lot, or jrebii, conceded no other right than that of having a distinct share in the open fields of the village. Each household possessed larger or smaller strips of ground in the different fields contained in the village area, and also had the right to mow a distinct portion of the village meadow, while the enjoyment of the waste and of the forest land was free to all the inhabitants of the volost, and no rules determined precisely the use which each householder was allowed to make of it.

You may see from what I have said that the run-rig system and equality of shares were as little known to the village communities of Old Russia, and specially of Muscovy, as to those of mediæval Germany or England. No better known was the correspondence which, according to Mr. Seebohm, existed in mediæval England between the quantity of ground owned by each household and the part it took in the ordinary labour of agriculture. Tillage performed by families possessing in common a "carruca," or sort of plough worked with three or four pairs of oxen, was quite unknown to my forefathers, who were in the habit of cultivating the ground with small ploughs, drawn very often by a single horse, a fact noticed in the epic poems, and particularly in the ballad, the chief hero of which is a simple peasant, Micoula Selianinovich. The same mode of tillage, I may add, is still in use among the peasants of Great Russia, where the ground is not nearly so heavy as is the black soil of our Southern provinces. The only thing that depended upon tenure of land was taxation, the householder paying a larger or smaller proportion of the land tax, according to the number of plough lands sown by his seed.

This is almost all we know of the free Muscovite village community. Our information is fuller as to the economic arrangements of those dependent communes, which were established on the possessions of the higher clergy and the monasteries. According to Professor Gorchacov, to whom we are indebted for a very circumstantial description of the inner life of these bodies, each manor regularly contained, next to the demesne land, a large area occupied by the dependent households. Each of these households was obliged to perform agricultural labour on the area belonging to the landlord, and in return possessed the right to a share in the autumn and spring fields, owned in common by the customary tenants of the manor. The existence of these two fields may be traced, at least in the central Governments of Russia, as far back as the beginning of the sixteenth century, as they are mentioned in a charter issued in the year 1511. The peasants had, before the end of that century, the right of free removal, the land quitted by a peasant household returning to the community of the villagers.* Besides the feudal lord, the state also had a claim on the community in the shape of a land tax, which the village assembly was itself authorised to collect. The area held by the village was accordingly divided into ploughs (*sochi*), and smaller divisions called *vuti*, which corresponded to a distinct part of the work of a plough. To make these financial arrangements clearer to an English public, I will say that the customary land of the village was divided into hides and virgates. The quantity of land contained in each virgate varied from one village to another, but the virgates of the same village were equal; in that respect the manor of mediæval England presents the greatest similitude to that of mediæval Russia. Both have this also in common, that each household was taxed according to the amount of arable land it owned. One household paid for one "vit," or virgate, another

* Gorchacov, "On the Land Possessions of Metropolitans, Patriarchs, and of the Holy Synod," p. 210.

for two, a third for half a virgate, and so on. The vit or virgate, just as in England, was not a number of fields surrounded by distinct boundaries, but a union of ideal shares in the different fields of the village. In the lands of the monastery of Constantine, for instance, the vit was, at least during the first part of the sixteenth century, equal to the right of occupying five desiatines in each of the three fields of the manor, a desiatine being equal to two acres. First introduced in order to secure an equal distribution of state taxation, the system of hides and virgates became later on the basis of the levy and distribution of feudal dues. Instances frequently occur in sixteenth century charters of the labour performed by each of the households being in direct ratio to the number of virgates, or viti, in its possession. Under such conditions, no equality could exist as to the amount of ground possessed by each villager. This equality was not demanded by anybody on account of the abundance of land and the facility of removal. The peasant who thought himself aggrieved could seek better terms on some neighbouring manor; removals were frequent, and the commune was always busy seeking for persons who might wish to become occupiers of the vacant ground of an abandoned virgate.

I shall proceed no further in the study of the social arrangements of the Russian manor because they appear to be, so far as the ownership of land is concerned, very like those of a free village. This is not surprising to one who knows the small difference which exists between the arrangements of a German manor, or Hof, and those of a free commune, or Dorf-gemeinde. The proprietor was too well pleased to see his yearly revenue guaranteed by the unpaid service of the villeins, to meddle with their internal arrangements. The villeins were accordingly allowed to choose their own executive officers, to have their elders, their "good men," or judicial assistants, and to apportion taxes and arrange the land ownership at their regular meetings, or folkmotes. Such being the case, I see no reason why the agrarian communism practised by the Russian peasantry should be much affected by their loose dependence upon the landlord, at least, before the time when serfdom was completely established and the peasant was prevented from removing from the manor.

The general characteristic of the old Russian community may be given in few words: it was a kind of ownership, based on the idea that the true proprietor of the land was none other than the commune. The rights of the commune to the soil occupied by the individual households appears in the indivisibility of the waste and forest lands, and in the fact that vacant shares are regularly disposed of by the commune, and that nobody is allowed to occupy a piece of ground lying within the limits of the village common, unless he is authorised by the local authorities. Arable land and meadows are, as a rule, in the hands of private households, which pay taxes and perform manorial labour in direct proportion to the amount of land they own. This ownership does not suppose the existence of certain limits which nobody is allowed to infringe. It implies only the right to have a definite share in the three fields, which constitute the agricultural area of the village. The shares are not equal, but differ in direct proportion to the payments which the household is called upon to make, partly to the State, and partly to the lord of the manor. Periodical redistributions are unknown, and no mention is made of the run-rig system of some modern English and Irish manors.

Thus constituted, the old Russian village community appears to be very like that of mediæval England with its system of open fields, its hides and virgates. It may be also compared to the German mark, so far as the mark is composed of a set of villages subdivided into units partly financial, partly territorial, called Hufen, and securing to their private holders, like the English virgates, the right to have a distinct share in the arable fields and in the meadows of the village.

Now that we are aware of the peculiar features of the mediæval village community, let us ascertain the reasons which have produced a complete revolution in its interior organisation by the introduction of the principle of equal division of the soil among its individual members, and the system of periodical allotments of ground in order to secure this equality.

Two facts seem to have contributed to this result; the first was the increase of population, which, as we have already shown in the instance of Little Russian communes, sooner or later induces the majority of persons holding small shares to force the rest to proceed to a redistribution of the soil. The other fact is the replacing of the land-tax by a sort of capitation tax, and the introduction of the principle of mutual responsibility, in matters of taxation. The first of these causes, increase of population, remained inoperative as long as the peasant retained the liberty of removing freely from one place to another. Much ground was lying waste. Landowners had no other thought than how to induce new colonists to settle on it; with this end in view they regularly freed them from all taxes for a period of three years. Those of the villagers, who thought themselves sacrificed to the interests of their neighbours could, therefore, easily find the land they wanted and that under very favourable conditions. They had only to leave the village they inhabited and seek for new homes, either on the still unoccupied steppes or on the manors possessed by the crown, the church, or the landed aristocracy.

Such was no longer the case when serfdom became a general rule, and the right of free migration was refused to the peasant. This happened during the period which extends from the end of the sixteenth to that of the seventeenth century. Two decades later followed the great change in matters of taxation when Peter the Great abolished the land-tax, and introduced the capitation-tax. This happened in the year 1719. Mutual responsibility of persons belonging to the same village was introduced, and both landlords and peasants were allowed to take preventive measures against those who might seek to escape the obligation of paying the personal tax by withdrawing from their habitations.

When this revolution was accomplished and each household began to be taxed, not according to the quantity of land it owned, but according to the number of persons attributed to it in the taxation returns, the grossest injustice would necessarily arise if the soil remained in the hands of its then holders. Complaints were therefore made, and petitions addressed, in which the old division of the village area was declared to be obnoxious, and an equality of shares was demanded as a necessary condition for the regular fulfilment by each village of its financial obligations towards the State. An instance of such a request is that presented by the peasants of the village of Petrovsk in the year 1725, in which they ask to have an equal share of land allotted to each member of the commune, all other kinds of allotment being contrary to justice. Similar demands must have been made repeatedly before the members of the legislative commission, convened by Catherine the Second, received orders to protest against the requirements of those who wanted all the land of a village to be distributed in equal shares according to the number of souls, notwithstanding that these lands had been fertilised by the work and private industry of the first settlers.*

For the reasons just mentioned, a redistribution of the land was made at least every time the Government revised its taxation returns; such revision occurring every nineteenth year. It was felt necessary to establish a direct relation between the number of persons living in a household, and the amount of land possessed by the household, and the fact, that the actual number of such persons did not correspond to those enumerated in the taxation-returns, even after the lapse of a few years, led some communes to have recourse to more frequent divisions. It is in this way that we may explain how it was brought about, that redistributions came to be made every sixth or even every third year. We hear of no yearly distribution because the three field system, still prevailing in Russia, required at least a three years' rotation of the crops. It was not always the country people who took the initiative in an equal re-allotment of the soil according to the number of persons taxed. Mr. Zabelin has brought forward instances, in which such allotments were made on the initiative of the lord of the manor, and Mr. Schimanov

* Petition presented by the peasants of the district of Vagra (Sergievitch, *Lectures and Inquiries*, p. 538).

has produced a curious case, in which such re-allotment was made by the direct order of a provincial Governor, who thought that justice required that the number of shares, owned by each household, should correspond to the number of souls composing it. This happened not longer ago than the second half of the seventeenth century in the Government of Kharkov, where inequality of shares had been up to that time the general rule. It is only by a general agreement between the people and the authorities that we can explain the rapid expansion of the present system. We do not find any trace of such redistributions before the end of the seventeenth century, when the borough of Schouia began to make new allotments of ground every ten years.*

Having now finished with the past history of the Russian village commune, we shall proceed to the study of its modern arrangements. These have formed the subject of very curious investigations, which have been carried on during the last few years by a number of young Russian economists, employed by the elective councils or "zemstva" of our provinces. Their work will probably be as valuable to coming generations, as that performed in England a century ago by Messrs. Sinclair and Marshall, or as that, which in our own day is still going on in India under the enlightened supervision of the

* Vladimirsky-Boudanov; "History of Russian Law," part ii. p. 196.

Indian Settlement Commissioners. I shall make free use of the rich material, which these skilful and untiring workers have accumulated, in order to present to you a picture of the prevailing system, the *mir* or village community of to-day.

According to the law of emancipation promulgated the 19th February 1861, the peasantry continue to possess an organisation quite distinct from that of the other classes of society. The ancient "volost" (or mark) is preserved or rather revived, and the villages are, as they were centuries ago, the administrative units of which it is formed. The volost and the village have alike their elected authorities, the right of election being based on a kind of universal suffrage, exercised by all the grown-up men of the community. But, differing in this from the French "commune," and the sections composing it, the Russian volost and village accord no right of suffrage to persons belonging to any other social position than that of peasant (krestianine, a word, the first meaning of which was Christian). A merchant or a nobleman may reside for years in a village; he will not thereby acquire any right to meddle with its internal administration. To explain the reason of such an anomaly, we must keep in view the circumstances under which the law of 1861 was promulgated. Its chief purpose was to liberate the serfs from their dependence on the landed aristocracy. The squire, the "pomeschick," was the enemy against whom they had to fight, and it was feared that he could easily regain the influence, which had lasted for centuries, if he and the persons in his service were allowed to have a vote in communal concerns. It was therefore to prevent a practical restoration of feudal power, that the upper classes were debarred from all interference in village matters. But the legislators forgot the dangers, which arise from the artificial isolation of an ill-educated class, both for itself and for the other orders of society. I know no country, in which the enlightened classes have so little opportunity of exercising that moral influence, without which no social progress can be really achieved. Not only the squire, be he a nobleman or a merchant, but also the parish priest (the pope), are excluded by law from the right to vote in the village assembly. Questions concerning public instruction and public health are daily discussed and settled by illiterate men, very often to the injury of the community, without any reference to the wishes and intentions of the more enlightened inhabitants, whose interference in such cases would be considered a direct infringement of the law. This is certainly a great wrong; a wrong which is clearly seen, both by society and by Government. The absenteeism of the higher classes and their dislike of that country life which is so familiar in England, certainly finds its chief root in what I may call the "privilegium odiosum" which is attached to the status. On the other hand, the ordinary peasant, left without that natural control and guidance which the enlightened classes are called upon to exercise towards the more ignorant, is naturally led to look for protection and help to those of his own rank who have succeeded in securing for themselves a certain amount of material wealth. This class of rich peasants, known under the name of "koulaks," which means a man knowing how to keep money in his own hands, is as a rule no better educated and far more selfish and immoral than the rest of the country people. The disintegrating influence, which such a class exercises, has been rightly recognised in the nickname with which the peasantry have dubbed its members, I mean that of "miroied" or "eaters of the *mir*." It is to such speculators and monopolists that the people are abandoned; it may be in the secret hope of rendering impossible any good understanding between them and the higher classes of the nation. For no doubt, such an understanding might become a serious obstacle in the way of the all-powerful bureaucracy, which rules over the masses with that insolence and harshness which are usually only met with in the relations of conquerors to a conquered nation. Instead of giving the higher classes their share in the affairs of the village, the Government has lately increased the number of administrative oppressors, by instituting a new office, that of "Commander of the district." This office is to be exclusively filled by members of the hereditary nobility. With no other control over them, than that of the Governor of the province, these newly-created officers are called upon to exercise a boundless authority, both executive and judicial, over the villages in their district. There is no judicial appeal against their doings, for they are at once police officers making their own by-laws, and magistrates authorised to decide questions of the infringement of these same by-laws; they are even the executioners of their own sentences, for the right of flogging on the spot, where the misdemeanour has been committed, is openly recognised as belonging to them.

It is not difficult to foresee the effect which the introduction of these new officers will have on the life of the people. Having been hitherto taught to look on the neighbouring squire as a stranger, they will now come to consider him as their natural enemy.

But let us go back to the study of the administrative organisation of the Russian *mir*.

Every village is authorised to have its popular assembly. This folkmote is the regular heir of the "vechas" and "koupas" still preserved, as we have seen, in the sixteenth and seventeenth centuries, among the South-Western communes of Russia, and, what is not less curious, also by the manorial system during the same centuries. When I say that all the adult members of the village are called upon to vote at these popular assemblies, I mean that this is the case in the majority of Russian villages, in which the inhabitants are likewise partners in the common lands of the village. It is not the case in the yearly increasing number of villages, in which the new-comers are only permitted to reside in the commune, but are prevented from sharing in the benefit which the commune derives from its property in land. In Germany and Switzerland, where centuries ago new-comers, known under the name of "Beisaszen" or "Hintersaszen," "domiciliès," "manants," &c., were allowed to settle side by side with the proprietors of the common land (the gemein-gut or allmend), two kinds of popular assemblies are known. The one is composed of all the adult inhabitants without distinction; the other of those who have a share in the common land. The first assembly makes by-laws, chooses officers, and passes measures which concern the common good. The second administers the lands of the village, appoints those entrusted with the care of them, and distributes to the several partners their shares in the commons. The laws of some Swiss cantons, therefore, establish a difference between the "politische Gemeinde," or commune, composed of all the male inhabitants, and the "bürgerliche Gemeinde," to which all the sharers in the common land, male and female alike, belong. Now this difference is unknown in Russia, where political rights are exclusively exercised by those inhabitants who are at the same time sharers in the common land.

The officer to whom the assembly entrusts the administration of the village is called the village elder. We find the same officer in the old Russian communes, both in the so-called "black hundreds"—in other words, in the villages inhabited by free-commoners—and also on the lands of manorial lords. Monastic charters, among other documents, very frequently mention the election of these officers, who are sometimes called, especially in the South-Western communes, "bourgmistr"—a name evidently derived from the German burgermeister, and showing, to a certain extent, the influence exercised by German municipal law on the local organisation of Lithuania and Little Russia.

It is the village elder, the starosta, who represents the commune in its relations with the district and provincial authorities. It is he who collects the taxes, exercises some supervision over the way in which the commune keeps in repair the roads and public buildings; sees that the law concerning obligatory fire insurance is obeyed, and carries into effect the various administrative enactments which the police authorities and the local assemblies of the zemstvo are very liberal in creating. But the most important functions of the commune, that of apportioning personal taxation and making periodical assessments of common land, are performed by the popular assembly or *mir*. Two-thirds of the whole number of voters are empowered to decide whether the proper time has come or not for a new general allotment. The same majority is also required whenever the division of the common land into private property has to be decided on.

Neither the assembly nor the village elder has any judicial authority; but the village elder exercises, to a certain extent, the functions of a public notary, for he gives legal validity to private documents and deeds by affixing to them the village seal.

A regular tribunal, a kind of court leet, is formed by the elective judges of the volost. This institution is an innovation introduced by the emancipation law, at least so far as it assigns, not to the village, but to the larger territorial district, the volost, the sole right of giving judicial decisions in civil suits and in misdemeanours among persons belonging to the peasant class. The peculiar feature of this tribunal is, that it is not bound to follow the prescriptions of law, but those of custom.

Russia, so far as I know, is the only European country, in which a sort of "personalitas legum" is still acknowledged, the peasants submitting to one complex code of legal rules, and the higher classes to another. What is no less characteristic is the fact that the customary law of the Russian peasant is alone the genuine Russian law—the law that is found in our ancient codes (such as the Pravda of Jaroslav, in the judicial charters of Novgorod and Pscov, in the statute of Lithuania, and in the codes of Ivan the Third and of Ivan the Terrible); whilst the volumes X. and XV. (so-called) of the general collection of laws (so the civil and criminal codes are designated in Russia) are a compound partly of

Russian, partly of French, partly of canon, Byzantine or even so-called natural law.

The only way to get rid of this dualism in matters of legislation would be to codify the customary law of Russia, introducing into it the changes required by the social development that has been already achieved by the higher classes. But such does not seem to be the opinion of the bureaucrats, to whom has been intrusted the difficult task of preparing the text of a new civil and criminal code. The books and pamphlets published by these modern Solons express an opposite view and would seem to justify the supposition that the double law will be scrupulously preserved, probably with the object of perpetuating the misunderstanding which already exists between the lower and higher classes of Russian society.

The volost has no assembly of its own, but it has its chief in the person of an elected elder "starschina," to whom the village elders are subject in all matters concerning the collection of taxes and the carrying into effect of laws and by-laws.

The little I have here said about the organisation of the village community will answer the end I have in view of placing clearly before you the economic arrangements made by the village in reference to the common lands. The relation in which the village stands to them is not that of proprietor. They belong according to law to the State alone. In those villages which are occupied by the so-called "State-peasants," that is the heirs of the serfs lately belonging to the "public domains," no means have been adopted to allow of the peasant becoming even in future the proprietor of the soil. Such, however, is not the case in those communes, which have been established on lands lately belonging to the nobility. As soon as the peasants on each estate have paid back the money advanced by the State to facilitate the acquisition of the land which the proprietor was forced to give up to them, they become the legal proprietors of the soil they now occupy. This payment may be made by the whole commune or by the separate households which belong to it. Five millions of roubles had been already devoted to this purpose up to the year 1881; later statistics are still wanting. Each time that the payment is made by a separate household, common property is of course superseded by private property and this enactment is rightly considered by Russian publicists as prejudicial to the further maintenance of agrarian communism.*

The commune exercises its proprietary rights in different ways. It keeps the waste-land and forests undivided, and makes periodical allotments of arable and meadow land. It was most prejudicial to the welfare of the peasants that the obligatory expropriation of 1861 did not extend to a part at least of

---

* Victor Prougavin, "The Village Community of Russia, according to Local Inquiries." Moscow, 1888, pp. 36, 37.

the waste-land of the manor, held previously to that date in common by the manorial lord and his serfs. We must acknowledge that in this respect the government of the old French monarchy, that of Louis XIII. and of Louis XIV., showed a far greater knowledge of the economic wants of the agricultural classes. The so-called "triages" secured to the peasants the right of exclusive enjoyment to at least a third of the manorial wastes and woods. Nothing which corresponds to those *triages* has been established in Russia. The result of this can be seen in the need which the peasant is under of diminishing year by year the number of his cattle, a condition of things which has already re-acted on the state of agriculture. In those cases where the village has had no access to the waste land, it has been obliged to carve out of its arable ground a special field to serve as a common pasture. But this can only be done where the allotments made out of the manorial land are of large extent. In the greater number of villages they have not amounted to more than three *dessiatines* a head, and the commoners have been forced to content themselves either with sending their cattle on to the "Lammas" lands, that is, the arable land after harvest, or with renting some pasture ground from a neighbouring squire.

As for the forests, allotments out of them were rarely made, at least in our Southern provinces where woods are scarce, and the peasant is quite dependent for his fuel on the squire, who takes advantage of this fact, and secures the regular performance of agricultural labour on his own domains in return for permission to use the dead wood which would otherwise lie unused. In the northern provinces allotments were frequently made of forests, and were sometimes treated as "assart lands." I make use of a term which is probably quite familiar to you, as it is frequently to be met with in English documents even of the first part of the present century. But for those who are not aware of its meaning I will add the following explanation. When population became dense, the village allowed new homesteads to be established in the middle of the forest; the trees were burned down, the roots seldom being removed, and the plough began to work in a region which had hitherto been accessible only to the axe. The area thus cleared for a time paid nothing to the State; but after a few years, three as a rule, it was annexed to the number of common lands which were burdened by personal taxes. The owners of these cleared lands received no allotments out of the common fields, but they regularly paid to the Government as much as the commoners of the same village.

We must now turn our attention to the way in which the arable land and the meadows are used. Equality being the chief aim of the members of the village community, its arable fields are as a rule very numerous. The commoners take into account both the differences in the fertility of the soil and the comparative advantages of its situation. Land which is either mountainous or distant from the village is not likely to produce the same revenue, or to be so easily cultivated as an equal area to it; the black soil is far more fruitful than the sandy or the clayey soil. The community, therefore, has a great number of "shots" or "furlongs,"* and in each of these *shots* every householder receives a number of strips equal to the number of the taxed persons in his household. You can easily imagine how scattered and intermixed are the possessions of each homestead. In cases where there is no great difference in the fertility of the soil, and the shots are consequently not very numerous, the community sometimes adopts a different method. The whole number of commoners is divided into "tythings," or decenas, and the fields are divided into as many parts as there are tythings. Each tything, or decena, then makes the division for itself. Lots are drawn to decide the order in which the strips must be distributed among the tythings and subdivided among the persons composing them.† Owing to the almost universal prevalence of the three-field system, the number of shots never falls below three.

The re-allotment of shares is of two kinds, partial

---

* I use terms made familiar by Mr. Seebohm; the ordinary term in use in Russia is "kon."

† Instances of such arrangements are given by Mr. Kapoustin, "A Review of Materials concerning the Village Community" (see a Russian magazine called *Russian Thought*, 1890, vol. i. p. 26).

and general. The first supposes the increase or diminution of the number of strips assigned to a household, consequent on an augmentation or decrease of the number of persons composing it. The second is equivalent to a complete change in the distribution of arable land among the commoners. It takes place at fixed periods, the shortest of which is three years, that being the time needed for a complete rotation of crops under the existing three fields' system; and the longest nineteen or more years—the number of years that separate the old census of a population from a new one. The number of shares allotted to each household either corresponds to the number of male persons for whom the household pays the personal tax, or to that of the souls actually living. Instances occur in which the villagers assign half shares to the women, or reserve certain shares unoccupied for the generation to come. As for the meadows, they are frequently mown in common, the hay being divided in equal parts among all the members of the commune. Very often, too, a yearly division takes place before harvest; account is taken of the greater or smaller distance of each meadow from the village, and of the quality of its grass, and then each commoner receives a strip in all and every one of the meadows. But I need not insist on the various aspects under which the system of re-allotments may present itself. It is not my purpose to give you a complete description of the various forms which the village community may take, but a general picture of all its characteristic features.

Amongst these I must place the control exercised by the village authorities over the performance at the proper time of each part of agricultural labour. The strips of the several households being scattered over the whole village area, and intermixed with those of their neighbours, the same system of agriculture must of necessity be followed by all. The system in use, as I have already told you, is that of the three fields, the winter, the summer, and the fallow; the fields becoming common pasture after the gathering in of the harvest. All agricultural labour must therefore begin and end at fixed periods, and the different households which constitute the village must do their ploughing, sowing, harrowing, mowing and reaping, precisely at the same time. The authorities of the village are empowered to insist upon this; the "Flurzwang," to use a well known German expression, is a necessary condition of this kind of agrarian communism, which is embodied in the system of the *mir*.

The performance at its proper time of each part of agricultural labour could not be attained if the commoners did not help one another in its accomplishment. This is the real origin of the obligation which compels every peasant to help his neighbours in mowing and reaping. This sort of communal help, regularly performed at harvest time, is known in Russia under the name of "village assistance."

It was under like conditions that the mediæval love-bones, or love boons (*angariæ autumni*), took their rise in England.

The feeling of mutual dependence, which has its origin in the common ownership and use of land, is the source from which springs another curious institution. Certain agricultural lands remain undivided and are cultivated by the combined work of the whole village; their yearly produce being regularly brought to the common store and equally distributed among all in case of dearth.

In Russian villages there are no special "poor" or "school lands" (Armen-und Schulgüter), similar to those of Switzerland or Germany, although the question has been recently raised as to the desirability of assigning certain shares of the common lands to the schoolmaster, he being authorised to cultivate them with the help of his pupils. This plan for turning the schoolmaster into an agricultural labourer belongs to the number of those measures, by which the reactionary party hope to prevent the badly paid village schoolmasters from becoming what they call "revolutionary dreamers." I am happy to say that it has not yet met with the support of the Government.

I now come to the capital question of the advantages and disadvantages, which the system of village communities presents, and which will of course exercise a decisive influence as to its future. There is no question so much discussed, and I may say, so often misunderstood by my countrymen, as that of the superiority or inferiority of the existing system in comparison with that of small holdings.

Both socialists and reactionaries have taken hold of the question, and both parties try to work it out in favour of their own systems. The value which they attach to the system of the *mir* differs considerably. What the socialists admire in it are the fruitful germs which they suppose it to contain of a future reorganisation of society on their own model. As to the Slavophils, they think it perfect in its present form, and never tire of repeating a saying which, with doubtful authenticity, is attributed to the great Cavour: "Russia will revolutionise the world with her system of the *mir*."

To an impartial observer the village communal system appears to be a compound of small advantages and great disadvantages; the advantages are rather of a moral, and the disadvantages of an economic character. It encourages, no doubt, to a much greater degree than the system of private holdings, the feeling of mutual interdependence and the inclination to mutual help, without which no society can exist. But it is a manifest error to speak of this system as a serious barrier to pauperism. For, although the commoner is prevented by law from alienating his share, he may, and often does, dispose of it in favour of some rich neighbour, who in time of want has offered to pay the amount of the commoner's taxes on condition of having the use of his land. If the Slavophils were right in their opinion, that, thanks to the system of the *mir*, pauperism was impossible in Russia, we should certainly not hear daily of the so-called "Koulaks" eating up the *mir*, or, what comes to the same thing, sacrificing the interests of the community to their own.

The economic disadvantages which the system presents are so evident that I need scarcely insist upon them. Instead of giving my own opinion on this subject, I prefer to quote the words of a Russian economist, who is far from belonging to the much decried Manchester School. "Agrarian communism, as it is applied in Russia," says Professor Ivanukov, "is a hindrance to the investment of capital in agriculture, and to the introduction of a more thorough, a better and more remunerative system of cultivation; for the strips belonging to this or that homestead will in case of each new division pass into strange hands, so that the peasant does not find it to his interest to lay out money which could only be recovered during a long term of possession." It is true that local inquirers have been able to produce several instances in which peasant commoners have introduced a somewhat thorough system of grass sowing;* but we must not forget that this has been done during a period when the readjustment of lots was rare.

We must not forget, too, one great disadvantage

---

* See the article written on this subject by a very promising Russian economist, Gourvitch, in the "Juridical Journal of 1890."

of the *mir* system, which consists in the fact that wherever it exists, the pieces of land belonging to the same holder are "scattered about on all sides of the township, one in this furlong and another in that, intermixed, and it might almost be said," writes Mr. Seebohm, "entangled together as though some one blindfold had thrown them about on all sides of him." *

Several Russian economists have shown that this defect is not peculiar to the *mir*, but is to be found in the system of small holdings,† as if these small holdings had not inherited it from their direct predecessor, the village community. What is, however, of far more importance than the opinion of this or that student of the *mir* is the fact that it is gradually and spontaneously breaking to pieces. There is no doubt that a general redistribution of shares has not taken place, at least in the more fertile area of the black soil, since the year of the peasants' emancipation. It is difficult to explain this solely by the dislike of the provincial and district administrators to the system; the unwillingness of the powerful minority of rich peasants to proceed to a new division is recognised on all sides, and quite suffices to explain the difficulties encountered in the way of a fresh readjustment. For we must remember that the law requires that two-thirds of the voters shall agree on any decision on this subject,

* "The English Village Community," Seebohm, p. 7.

† See Posnikoff's "Common Ownership of Land," part ii.

and the Koulaks, although in a minority, are sure to have influence enough among the poorer peasants, who are their debtors, to obtain their own way in a folkmote.

The fact that a movement in favour of a re-division of the common lands has arisen in the northern and central provinces, where the soil is poor, and the income which the peasant receives from his share does not cover the amount of the taxes he has to pay, can certainly not be adduced in favour of the idea of a further spontaneous development of Russian agrarian communism.

The majority of the peasants insist on such a readjustment, so that they may have fewer taxes to pay, and not because they long to see the great principle of equality become the ruling power of the world. If we wish to point to a really spontaneous movement in the sphere of land-tenure, it must certainly be to that which has induced thousands of peasants to pay back the money which was advanced to them by the Government in the year of their emancipation to enable them to become the free proprietors of the soil. I have already mentioned the fact that five million roubles have been repaid to the Crown; it is interesting to note the rate at which this repayment has been made. From 1861 to 1868, according to Mr. Keuszler, the amount of money paid by persons wishing to exchange their common rights for private property, hardly formed the seven-hundredth part of the whole sum. From

1868 to 1872 it had amounted to 10 per cent.; from 1873 to 1877 to 33½ per cent.; the rest of the sum, or 55 per cent., having been paid back during the years 1877 to 1881.*

If this steady increase is not considered a conclusive proof, I must decline to bring forward any other, not even the disappearance of village communities in the neighbourhood of the larger towns, such as St. Petersburg, Moscow, and even Voroneg, owing to the fact that in their neighbourhood high farming pays best, and that this high farming is impossible without a change in the system of land property.

How long village communities will exist is not a question easy to answer. The Government may certainly prevent for a time their dissolution by some artificial measures, like those taken in relation to the undivided household. A proposal has even been made to declare that the common-land shall not become private property even after the repayment of the whole sum which its holder owes to the Government. Such a measure might, indeed, long arrest the spontaneous movement which produces the dissolution of this archaic form of agrarian communism.

If left to itself, it will certainly be maintained in those remote parts of Russia where the population is still so small as to retard agricultural progress;

* Keuszler, "Zur Geschichte und Kritik des bäuerlichen Gemeindebesitzes in Russland," Dritter Theil, 1887, p. 82.

but it is likely soon to disappear in the manufacturing districts, where the peasant passes more time in the factory than in the fields, and where, when he leaves his old home, he has to find, and that ofttimes under very unsatisfactory conditions, some partner to perform his share of field labour. It is also more than probable that the South of Russia, the true granary of the Empire, will soon become a country of private ownership in land. The system of the *mir*, as I have already said, is in more than one part of this district a comparatively modern innovation. The Little Russian is too fond of independence and self-control to acquiesce in a system which confines his industry in every direction.

The village community, that venerable survival of an epoch closely akin to the patriarchal, will disappear in Russia, as it already has disappeared in other countries in Europe—in England, Germany, and Switzerland. It will give way to private property in land, unless, and this is not very likely under present conditions, it be completely transformed by the extension of communistic principles to capital. Those who, like myself, do not believe in the possibility of leaps and bounds in matters of social progress, will probably consider that such a state of things belongs to the number of those dreams, the practical realisation of which is to be looked for only in a remote future.

# LECTURE IV.

## OLD RUSSIAN FOLKMOTES.

It is a common saying among the Russian Conservatives, who have lately been dignified in France by the name of "Nationalists," that the political aspirations of the Liberals are in manifest contradiction with the genius and with the historical past of the Russian people.

Sharing these ideas, the Russian Minister of Public Instruction Count Delianov, a few years ago ordered the Professors of Public Law and of Legal History to make their teaching conform to a programme in which Tzarism, the unlimited power of the Russian emperors, was declared to be a truly national institution.

Some of the professors who refused to comply with this order were called upon to resign, others were simply dismissed from their chairs. The question I am about to discuss in this and the following lecture is, whether this theory bears the test of history. Is it true that Russian autocracy is a thoroughly national institution, the roots of which are found in the remotest period of Russian history?

Is it the fact that no folkmotes and no representative institutions ever existed in the eastern part of Europe, and that the Byzantine principle of an unlimited monarchical power, having no other source but its divine right derived from God himself and being responsible to no one but Heaven, has been always recognised by my countrymen?

I shall begin by saying that, had such been the case, the historical development of Russia would form a monstrous anomaly to the general evolution of political institutions, at least among people of Aryan blood.

It is not before an Oxford audience that I need recall this well-established fact, that in earlier times the assembly of the people, the Folkmote, shared in the exercise of sovereign power side by side with the elected head of the nation, whatever may have been his title. Professor Freeman and Sir Henry Maine have left no possibility of doubt on this point; the first, when treating of the Greeks, Romans, and Germans; the second, in relation to the ancient Celtic population of Ireland. The barrier of language, of which Sir Henry Maine so often complained to me, prevented these two eminent scholars from completing their comparative study of early political organisation by a minute investigation of that of the mediæval Slavs; but recent researches, carried on both in Russia and in Poland, Bohemia and Servia, permit us to extend to Slavonic nations the general conclusions which have been arrived at by those English scholars, who have taken as their basis a careful study of Hellenic, German, and Celtic law.

Byzantine chronicles, which contain the earliest information on the social and political condition of the Slavs, are unanimous in the assertion that the Slavonic people knew nothing of a strongly centralised autocratic power. "From the remotest period," says Procopius, a writer of the sixth century, "the Slavs were known to live in democracies; they discussed their wants in popular assemblies or folkmotes" (chapter xiv. of his "Gothica seu Bellum Gothicum"). Another authority, the Byzantine Emperor Mauriquius, when speaking of the Slavs, writes as follows: "The Slavs like liberty; they cannot bear unlimited rulers, and are not easily brought to submission" ("Strategicum," chap. xi). The same language is used also by the Emperor Leo. "The Slavs," says he, "are a free people, strongly opposed to any subjection" ("Tactica seu de re militari," ch. xviii. 99).

Passing from these general statements to those which directly concern some definite Slavonic people, we will first of all quote the Latin Chronicles of Helmold and Dithmar of Merseburg, both of the eleventh century, in order to give an idea of the political organisation of the Northern Slavs dwelling on the south-eastern shore of the Baltic. Speaking of one of their earliest chiefs named Mistiwoi, Helmold says that he, the chief, once complained to the whole assembly of the Slavs of an injury he had received (Convocatis omnibus Slavis qui ad orientem habitant, intimavit eis illatam sibi contumeliam).

The Russian scholars who have made a special study of the history of those Slavonic tribes who were so early Germanised, give us a description of the proceedings and functions of their popular assemblies. The folkmote was convened in an open place. In Stettin the market-place was furnished for this purpose with a kind of stand from which the speakers addressed the multitude. The folkmotes were not periodical assemblies, but were convened as often as there was some question of State which needed public discussion.

It is well known that the privilege enjoyed in our days by the majority was quite unknown to the primitive folkmotes. In early times the decisions of the people were unanimous. This does not mean that it was always easy to arrive at a general agreement. Opinions were certainly as divided then as they are now. What is meant is only this—that, in case of difference of opinion, the minority was forced to acquiesce in that of the majority, unless it could succeed in persuading the majority that they were in the wrong In the Chronicle of Dithmar of Merseburg the "unanimous vote" is distinctly stated to be a peculiarity of the primitive Slavonic folkmotes·

"Unanimi consilio," says this author, "ad placitum suimet necessaria discutientes in rebus efficiendis *omnes concordant.*" In case some one refused to acquiesce in the common decision, he was beaten with rods. If any opposition to the vote of the majority arose after the assembly had been held, the dissentient lost all his property, which was either taken from him or destroyed by fire, unless he was ready to pay a certain amount of money, varying according to his rank. The unanimous vote is very often mentioned by contemporary chroniclers, who for this purpose employ the following expressions: "Remota controversia," or "quasi unus homo."* The matters discussed at these early Slavonic folkmotes were of a great variety: the election or the dethroning of a prince, decisions about going to war or making peace, are more than once mentioned by contemporary authors as the direct work of these assemblies.

If we turn our attention to the study of the earliest period in the history of Bohemian political institutions, we shall see the development of facts similar or quasi-similar to those just mentioned. The Bohemian folkmote, the "*snem,*" as it was called, is known to Latin chroniclers under the names of *conventus*, *generale colloquium*, or *generalis curia*. Persons of different estates or orders constituted the assembly. The chronicles mention, as a rule, the presence of the *majores natu*, of the *proceres* and *comites*, as also that of the higher

---

* Herbord, ii. 15–30.

clergy, *in clero meliores;* but in addition we find at these meetings, at least as far back as the end of the eleventh century, the common people, the *populus; Bohemorum omnes, Bohemicæ gentis magni et parvi, nobiles et ignobiles.* In the year 1055 the people are especially mentioned as taking part in the election of a duke, and in 1068 and 1069 as engaged in the nomination of a bishop. In 1130 the Duke Sobeslav convened an assembly of 3000 persons, *nobiles et ignobiles,* to judge those who had conspired against him. At a later period, after the beginning of the twelfth century, the common people disappear from these assemblies, and the *proceres* and *majores natu* remained alone with the high clergy to discuss the affairs of the State. But in the early days with which we are at present concerned the constitution of the Bohemian *snem* was not very unlike that of an ordinary folk-mote, to which all classes of society were equally summoned. Like the folkmotes of the Baltic Slavs, the Bohemian *generalis conventus* was not a periodical assembly. Like them also, its decisions were the result of a unanimous consent, a fact which is shown by the contemporary documents, when they state that this and that matter have been settled at the assembly "*communio consilio et voluntate pari*" (Cosmus of Prague, ii. 87), or even more explicitly, "de consensu omnium," "unanimiter."

The election first of the duke and later on of the king, the nomination of the bishop, the confirmation or rejection of the laws proposed by the king and his council, the judicial decision of certain exceptionally important cases, such were the regular functions of the Bohemian folkmote. You will have no difficulty in seeing that these functions are the same as those of the popular assemblies of the Baltic Slavs.

In Poland, the folkmotes, known under the name of *congregationes generales*, sometimes also under that of *conciones*, *colloquia*, or *consilia*, were in early days composed not only of the higher orders of society, but also of the common people. The Latin Chronicle of Gallus mentions an occasion on which king Boleslaus "imprimis majores et seniores civitatis, deinde totum populum in concionem advocavit." The meaning of this quotation leaves no doubt as to the popular character of these early Polish political assemblies. In no Slavonic state was this popular character so early lost as in Poland. As early as the beginning of the thirteenth century the higher nobility and clergy, the "milites" and the knights, begin to be the only constitutive parts of the Polish "general council."

The other feature of the primitive folkmote, the unanimous vote, was much better preserved by the Polish parliament. From the earliest times down to the fall of their political independence, the Poles remained faithful to this very incongruous system. The "*liberum veto*," the right of each member to make null and void by his single opposition the decisions of the entire assembly, became through the interference of foreign States one of the best means of keeping in check the political activity of the nation. By this veto, Russian, Austrian, and Prussian intrigues more than once prevented the passing of laws and measures, which might have preserved the independence of the country. That the *liberum veto* had its roots in the most remote period of Polish history may be shown by quotations like the following. According to the chronicle of Cromer, the Polish throne had been offered to the half mythical Cracus, "*una sententia*," *i.e.*, by the unanimous decision of the people, who had, as we know, no other means of manifesting their feeling than the folkmote. The same unanimous consent is mentioned by another chronicle on the occasion of an election which took place in 1194.

The legal power of the Polish general council was identical with that of the Bohemian *snem*. It elected the chief ruler of the land and entered into written covenants with him; it discussed questions of international policy, expressed its opinion on matters of taxation, gave its sanction to the legal enactments of the king, the so-called *statuta* and *constitutiones*, and from time to time it exercised judicial authority in certain exceptionally important civil cases. In a word, it possessed the same multiplicity of powers which we have noticed when studying the powers of the Bohemian folkmote.

Hitherto we have consulted only the history of the Northern and Western Slavs. Let us now turn to that of the Southern Slavs. The democratic element is less prominent in the constitution of the ancient Servian and Croatian folkmotes. At a very early period the high nobility and clergy took possession of the various powers of the popular assembly. But this does not mean that no documentary evidence has reached us concerning the part which the lower classes of society, at least in Croatia, were anciently called upon to play in the political organisation of the country. The old Croatian chronicle explicitly states that in the time of Svonomir, the first elected Croatian chief, the "*Ban*," the national assembly known in later times under the name of "*Sobor*," was composed not only of the higher orders (viteze, barune, vlasnike), but also of the common people (puk zemlie). The same common people is mentioned by the Latin chronicle as having had its share in the election of this first Ban, who was chosen "concordi totius cleri et populi electione." This happened in the second half of the eleventh century (1076). During the following centuries the nobility, and among them the higher class of nobles represented by seven Bans, alone had a direct influence on the nomination of the Croatian king. But the memory of old days, when the people chose their rulers, was still preserved down to the end of the fifteenth century, as may be seen from the following words of a charter issued in 1490 by King Vladislas the second: "Domini, prelati et barones, cæterique primores et universi incolœ regni, ad quos scilicet jus eligendi novum regem ex vetustissimâ regni ipsius libertate et consuetudine devolutum exstiterat . . . . oculos mentis ipsorum in nos conjecerunt."

The texts already quoted establish the fact that like other Slavonic assemblies, the Sobors of Croatia were ignorant of the rights of the majority and insisted on the necessity of a unanimous decision. Expressions like "concordi electione," "omnibus collaudantibus," and the complete absence of any information concerning decisions taken by a majority of voters, leave no doubt on this point. The same texts mention several of the functions which the Sobor was called upon to exercise, and first among these was the election of the political heads of the nation, who might be simple bans or kings. Questions of peace and war were also settled by this assembly.

But the chief occupation of the Sobor was of a legislative character. From time to time the chronicles state that "many good laws have been made" by this or that assembly, and Professor Bogisic has succeeded in tracing a whole list of the different statutes resulting from their deliberations.

The existence of these national councils did not prevent the people of different localities from meeting in some kind of provincial assemblies, and from exercising in them even legislative functions. An instance of this fact is presented by the island of Vinodol, the inhabitants of which in 1288 met in a kind of local folkmote—at which certain men were chosen to make a general codification of old laws, the memory of which was still preserved. In this way was formed the celebrated statute of Vinodol, one of the chief sources of information as to the early law of the Southern Slavs.

The Servian States-General, although much less democratic than the Croatian, merit our attention on account of the great influence which they exercised on the management of public affairs. It is true that the Servian Sobor is rather a council of the higher orders, a sort of Anglo-Saxon Witenagemote, than a folkmote or popular assembly. The third estate was not admitted to its meetings either as a body or by representation, and one of the paragraphs of the celebrated code of Stefan Douschan (fourteenth century) even strictly forbids the peasants to meet in political assemblies. But the lower nobility, who afterwards played such a prominent part in the destinies of the Polish nation, regularly sat in those meetings side by side with the king, his council, the superior officers of State, the patriarch, the ecclesiastical synod, and the members of the higher nobility. These orders taken together exercised pretty nearly all the functions of sovereignty. They made legal enactments, such as the code just mentioned, and they were the authors of the different amendments introduced into it in the course of time. They very often elected the king, and sometimes dethroned him. The archbishop and the provincial governors were also chosen by the Sobor, which likewise disposed of the public lands, and discussed the most important matters of civil and ecclesiastical government.

This rapid and rather superficial sketch of the early political institutions of the Slavs, may at least serve to show how considerable was the influence which the higher orders of society, and very often the common people, exercised in the management of the Slavonic State. My necessarily dry exposition of ancient chronicles and charters, cannot fail to recall the well-known passage in the "Germania" of Tacitus: "De minoribus principes consultant, de majoribus omnes." Like the old Germanic folkmote the Slavonic was a sort of supreme council, convened on certain exceptionally important occasions. During an interregnum all authority passed into its hands, and it was accordingly empowered to choose the future ruler of the land, and to declare under what conditions he was to be admitted to the exercise of the sovereign power. In the ordinary course of public affairs, the folkmote discussed important matters of civil, and in some countries even of ecclesiastical government. It pronounced on questions of war and peace, controlled the exercise of the legislative authority, and was sometimes even directly engaged in the making of new, and the codifying of ancient laws. Although its authority was less prominent in executive and judicial matters, yet it very often exercised the supreme right of dethroning a king, and of judging persons accused of high treason.

When we call to mind these facts, the idea of an early Russian autocracy, admitting of no control on the part of the governed, will certainly appear to us to be in direct contradiction not only of the general evolution of political institutions, but also of its usual form among Slavonic nations. We must refuse to accept an anomaly unless it is established on the authority of well-authenticated historical facts. But no such facts can be produced. The Russian chronicles, in which, from the want of other sources of information, we are obliged to seek for the chief elements of a general theory of ancient Russian political institutions, show us a state of things, which has nothing in common with absolute monarchy. On the first pages of the chronicle attributed to the monk Nestor, the Eastern Slavs are spoken of as possessing a sort of "gens" organisation; "each one living with his kindred, and these kindreds occupying distinct territorial districts." (Kojdo s svoim rodom i na svoich mestech, kojdo vladeiusche rodom svoim.) In the sentence just quoted, the chronicler describes the social organisation of the most enlightened tribe of the Eastern Slavs, the Polians, and immediately afterwards he speaks of three brothers and their sister, who exercised in common some sort of political authority over the tribe. According to this chronicler, the direct descendants of these brothers ruled over the Polians. It is also recorded of the Drevlians, another Slavonic tribe, that it had its own prince,

Mal. but the Polians and the Drevlians seem to have been the only tribes living under monarchical rule. The rest of the Slavonic tribes established in Russia are represented to us as having no princes, but as living divided into clans or "gentes," which were often at war one with another (vsta rod na rod), a state of things which at length induced them "to seek a foreign prince (kniaz) to command and judge them according to justice." The establishment of monarchical power thus appears to have been the direct result of a free decision on the part of the people. The chronicle speaks of the tribes, which sent for a foreign prince, as having previously assembled together (snidoschasia vkoupe, sobravschesia). This means that the decision to call in a foreign prince was the work of a folkmote. Such is the first mention we possess of a Russian popular assembly. The facts I have recorded happened in the second half of the ninth century, in the year 862. Alluding to them, the chronicle of Sousdal, under the year 1176, makes the following general statement. "The inhabitants of Novgorod, of Smolensk, of Kiev, and of Poloczk, and of all the principalities (volosti) of Russia, were from the beginning, and are still, in the habit of meeting at folkmotes as at a sort of council." The term employed to designate the folkmote is that of *veche* from the verb *veschat*, to announce, to declare. According to the sentence just quoted, the veche may be traced from the oldest period of our national existence. This is directly confirmed, in relation to the Polians, by the following statement: "In the years next following," says Nestor, speaking of the end of the ninth century, "they thought in common (sdoumavsche) and decided to pay to the Chasars a certain tax, the amount of which was one sword from every hearth." The Drevlians are also spoken of by the chronicle as having on one occasion "thought in common with their prince Mal," and decided to slaughter the son of Rurik, Igor. Now, this "thinking in common" of a whole tribe with its political head, can only mean that the prince consulted the folkmote, and with its help arrived at a definite decision.

A peculiar feature of the oldest Russian folkmotes, a feature which totally disappears by the end of the tenth century, is, that they are the assembly of a whole tribe, sometimes even of several tribes, and not of the inhabitants of one single urban district. The Chronicle of Nestor speaks of the Polians, the Drevlians, the Krivichs, the Sever, and such like people, as of persons coming together, consulting one another and "accomplishing certain acts in common." I have already said that these were separate tribes, each one subdivided into kindreds or "gentes" (rodi). Such being the case, the veche of the early days of Russian historical development, was a kind of tribal assembly very like those which Cæsar and Tacitus found among the ancient Germans.

With the beginning of the eleventh century, the Russian folkmote or veche acquired a new character, when the chief cities of Russia, the political centres of more or less independent states, obtained their separate assemblies. The chronicles mention on different occasions the veches of Belgorod, of Vladimir in Volhynia, of Berestie, of Riazan, Mourom, and Pronsk, of Smolensk, Poloczk and Koursk, of Rostov, Sousdal, Pereiaslavl and Vladimir on the Kliasm, besides those of Kiev, Novgorod, Pscov, and Viatka.

If we inquire into the internal constitution and functions of the veche, we shall have no difficulty in ascertaining that in both these points the Russian folkmotes did not essentially differ from those of other Slavonic nations.

The chronicles, when they speak of those summoned to these assemblies, briefly note the presence of all the citizens of a definite urban division. Expressions such as the following are also more than once met with in the course of the narrative: "the men of our land," "the whole land of Galich," and so on. Hence, it is evident that we have to deal with a thoroughly democratic assembly. But it does not follow that all the inhabitants of the city were summoned. The veche was not so much an assembly of the whole people as that of the heads of families, or rather of the natural chiefs of Slavonic house communities known to the earliest code of Russia, the Pravda of Jaroslav, under the name of "verv."

On several occasions the unknown authors of

Russian chronicles seem to imply that the men assembled at the folkmote made certain engagements, not only on their own behalf but also on that of their children. For instance, "the men of Kiev, in folkmote assembled," declare in 1147, that they will fight against the House of Oleg, one of the branches of the dynasty of Rurik, not by themselves alone, but also by their children. This declaration clearly shows that children did not appear at a Russian folkmote, but that their absence was solely caused by their personal dependence on the head of the undivided family. We may, therefore, infer that all those who were not free to dispose of themselves were excluded from the veche; and such was the case as regarded certain members of undivided households and those who had forfeited their liberty through war or debt. In a society based, like the old Russian, on the principle of blood relationship, undivided households must have been numerous, and the fact that the heads of these households were alone summoned naturally diminished the number of persons composing the veche. It may, therefore, be easily understood how a large square such as those on which the princely palaces of Novgorod or of Kiev were built, was quite able to contain an entire assembly, notwithstanding the fact that the citizens were not the only persons admitted to the meetings of the veche, for the suburbs and even the neighbouring townships had the right to have an equal share with them on the management of public affairs.

The chronicles very often mention the fact of the "black people," "the smerds," and the so-called "bad peasants" (terms designating the agricultural population of the country) being present at the veche. The urban district was as a rule very large, the lands owned by the citizens in some cases extending to hundreds and even thousands of miles outside the city wall. In order to preserve these widely scattered possessions, the city often built fortresses, which in case of war offered a refuge to the inhabitants of the surrounding country. In time of peace these fortified places answered another purpose; markets were regularly held in them and hence in course of time artisans and merchants were induced to choose them for their settled abode. The population increased day by day, the fortress became surrounded by suburbs, and a new city appeared where originally there had been nothing but a wooden fence with a moat or ditch around it. The inhabitants of this new city had generally the right to appear at the veches of the metropolis, but they usually preferred meeting at assemblies of their own. The roads being bad and not always safe, they did not see what was to be gained by a long journey, but chose rather to stay at home and hold their own folkmotes from time to time.

The chronicles of Sousdal seem to imply that the decisions of the local folkmotes did not, as a rule, differ from those of the metropolis. "What has been established by the oldest city, is maintained by its boroughs." Such are the words in which the chronicle expresses the mutual relations of the metropolis and the daughter towns. The real meaning of the sentence is not at all that of dutiful subjection on the part of the new town towards the mother city. The writer merely wishes to suggest the idea of a good understanding between the metropolis and the boroughs it has built. This good understanding was not always maintained, and on more than one occasion the borough came to a decision the reverse of that of the chief city. A similar disagreement occurred more than once between different quarters (konzi) of the same city. Such was often the case at Novgorod, divided as it was into five different administrative districts or wards, which more than once held their own separate folkmotes and opposed the decisions of the general assembly. Such a misunderstanding sometimes ended in open war, the minority refusing to submit to the decision of the majority.

This fact alone shows that the Russian veches admitted no other mode of settling public affairs than that of unanimous decision. It has been already shown that this mode was general amongst Slavonic peoples. A few quotations will prove its existence among the Eastern Slavs. Whenever the chronicler has occasion to speak of one of their decisions he employs such expressions as the following: "It was established by all the oldest and all the youngest men of the assembly that," &c.; "all were unanimous in the desire"; "all thought and spoke as one man," &c.

If unanimity could not be arrived at, the minority was forced to acquiesce in the decision of the greater number, unless it could persuade the members of the majority that they were wrong in their opinion. In both cases the veches passed whole days in debating the same subjects, the only interruptions being free fights in the street. At Novgorod, these fights took place on the bridge across the Volchov, and the stronger party sometimes threw their adversaries into the river beneath. A considerable minority very often succeeded in suspending the measure already voted by the veche, but if the minority was small, its will had soon to yield to open force.

The competence of the Russian folkmote was as wide as that of similar political assemblies among the Western and Southern Slavs. More than once it assumed the right of choosing the chief ruler of the land; but it was not an unrestricted right which they enjoyed, the choice being confined to members of the family of Rurik; for the Russians considered that outside Rurik's dynasty, no one had a right to exercise sovereign power. The folkmote was merely empowered to give its preference to some distinct line of the house of Rurik, for instance to that directly descending from Vladimir Monomach, from which the veche of Kiev elected its rulers. It was also free to pronounce in favour of a younger member of Rurik's family, notwithstanding the candidature of an older one. The choice made was often in open contradiction of the legal order of succession maintained by the dynasty of Rurik. This order was very similar to the Irish law of tanistry, according to which the Irish crown devolved upon the oldest representative of the reigning family. In practice it generally meant the succession of the deceased's next brother, not that of his eldest son. The strict application of this law of tanistry would have necessitated a constant change in the person of the ruler, not only in Kiev, which was for a long time considered the most important principality of Russia, and which was, therefore, the appanage of the chief representative of the dynasty, but also in the other Russian dukedoms, which were subdivided into a great number of secondary principalities. Open force had very often to decide which of the two systems, that of free election or that of legal succession, was to prevail.

Whatever was the issue of such a struggle the new ruler was only admitted to the exercise of sovereign power after having subscribed a sort of contract by which he took upon himself the obligation of preserving the rights of those over whom he was called to rule. These very curious documents, known under the name of "riad," have unfortunately been preserved in only one of the Russian principalities, that of Novgorod,—a fact which has induced many scholars to believe that this right of covenanting with the duke was limited to this Northern principality. Professor Sergievitch, the well-known Professor of Legal History in the University of St. Petersburg, was the first to prove by a considerable number of quotations from Russian chronicles, that covenants like that of Novgorod were known all over Russia. More than once mention is made of a prince securing the throne by a compromise with the men of Kiev ('s liudmi Kieva outverdisia). These compacts or covenants between prince and people, so far as they are known to us by the few examples among the archives of Novgorod, were a kind of constitutional charter securing to the people the free exercise of their political rights, such as the right of the folkmote to discuss public affairs and to elect the ruler of the State. This latter right had been already guaranteed to Novgorod by a general assembly of Russian dukes held in 1196. We read in the text of the decisions come to by this princely congress; "All the dukes recognise the liberty of Novgorod to choose her ruler wherever she likes." Other constitutional restraints on princely power are—no declaration of war without "Novgorod's word"; no foreigner to be nominated to the post of provincial governor (volostel); no public official to be dismissed without legal cause, acknowledged to be such by the decision of a Court of law. Thus the principle according to which most English officials hold office "during good behaviour" was already recognised in Russian principalities in the middle of the thirteenth century. This efficient mode of securing the independence and dignity of public officials has been completely abolished in later days under the Tzars and Emperors, although once more in 1863 its necessity was admitted by the legal enactments of Alexander II. Unfortunately no attention is any longer paid to the promises given to this effect by the codes of civil and criminal procedure, and many a judge has been removed in recent times by a simple order of the Minister of Public Justice.

Returning to the constitutional guarantees secured by the new ruler to his future subjects, I must point out that those already mentioned seem to have been common to all the different principalities of Russia. The same cannot be said of the following two: first, the obligation to judge nobody without the assistance of a special officer, called the posadnik, and secondly, the right of the folkmote to choose this official, a right which first appeared in the beginning of the twelfth century. These exceptions once made, we have the right to say that the compacts entered into by the people of Novgorod with their future ruler, give us a fair idea of the relative strength of the prince and of the popular assembly all over Russia.

Our review of the agreement signed by the prince on his accession to the throne has already revealed to us some of the functions of the veche. Questions of war and peace were regularly decided by it. No war could be begun but with the consent of the people, because, in the absence of a regular army, the prince could levy no other force but that of the militia. Treaties of peace and alliance were also signed in the name of the prince and people, as may be seen from the following words used in the treaty of Igor with the Byzantine empire in 945; "This treaty has been concluded by the Grand Duke of Russia, by all the dukes whatsoever and by all the people of the Russian lands." Sometimes, it is true, the duke decided on going to war against the wish of his people, but in such a case he had to rely exclusively on his own military followers, his so-called "drougina," an institution very like the old German "comitatus" (Geleit). As long as the system of land donations remained unknown, and the duke had no other property to distribute among his followers but that taken in time of war, the drougina or comitatus was far from being numerous. Hence the duke was forced to ask the veche for assistance whenever he thought himself obliged to go to war. The veche either agreed to his demand and ordered the levy of military forces, or refused all help; in the latter case the duke had no other alternative but to abandon his project entirely, or to resign his throne. The control in matters of peace and war was maintained by the people so long as the duke had no other troops than the militia. But a kind of regular army had been created by the end of the thirteenth century, owing to the custom of rewarding military service by grants of land. The so-called "pomestnaia" system, which was similar to the Carlovingian system of "benefices," produced in Russia effects similar to those produced in France. The popular militia was superseded by a sort of feudal army, paid not in money but in land. In case of war the duke was not so much interested in having the acquiescence of the people as that of the "men of service," *slougilii liudi*, who constituted his military force, and corresponded somewhat to the knights in feudal England. This change, as we shall hereafter see, had a great influence on the future destiny of the Russian folkmote.

Another function of the folkmote, which appears to be peculiar to the Northern principalities, and especially to those of Novgorod and Pscov, is that of legislation. That the legislative functions of the veche were unknown in the Southern principalities of Russia may be seen from the fact, that no mention is made of them in the most ancient code of the country. The Pravda of Jaroslav in its different versions shows no trace of the interference of the people in matters of legislation; it is the exclusive work of the duke and his councillors. The few amendments introduced into this legal code during the first part of the twelfth century have also no other source but the express desire of the dukes and the decisions of their Doumas or Councils.

The exercise of legislative power by the veches of Novgorod and of Pscov, at least during the fourteenth and fifteenth centuries, is illustrated by two judicial charters, those of 1397 and of 1471, which, as is evident from their contents, were drawn up by the popular assembly. The charter of Pscov plainly states in one of its later versions (that of 1467), that whenever the posadnik, the supreme judge elected by the people, has to decide a case to which no existing law applies, he must consult the assembly of the people. The same veche had the right to annul every article of the judicial charter which no longer met with its approval. Mention of this right is made in the charter itself.

As to judicial powers, they remained unknown to the veche, at least in the Western and Southern principalities of Russia, which knew no other judges than the duke and the officers whom he appointed. I do not allude to those arbitrators to whom private persons frequently had recourse to settle their differences.

But in Novgorod, the fact of the election of the chief judge, the posadnik, by a popular vote, shows that the people were not indifferent to the exercise of judicial power. Appointed as he was by the folkmote, the posadnik could be judged by no other tribunal than the folkmote itself. Cases of high treason were also referred to the popular assembly just as they were in Poland and Bohemia.

What has been stated establishes beyond a doubt the great extent of the rights and privileges belonging to the folkmote in the Northern principalities of Russia. The same cannot be said of some Western principalities, such as those of Volhynia and Galicia.

The example of Poland, where the aristocracy was very powerful, induced the boyars of those two countries to make more than one attempt to concentrate in their own hands the chief rights of sovereignty. The large estates which they possessed and the considerable revenues, which the rich black soil of the country yearly secured to them, greatly favoured their oligarchical aspirations. In 1210, they seem to have attained their ends. The dynasty of Rurik had ceased to rule over the country, and a boyar, a member of the local aristocracy, had been raised to the throne. But his rule did not last long. His contemporaries, the other rulers, looked upon his elevation as illeg , and the King of Poland was the first to declare that a boyar had no right to occupy a throne. To oppose the oligarchy of the boyars Duke Daniel, in 1230, convened the popular assembly, the veche, and with the help afforded him by people, fought the army of the boyars and reduced them to obedience. This is, however, the only case in which the veche seems to have played any part in the political history of the country. The power of the nobles prevented any further development in that direction, and when the principality passed into the hands of the King of Poland, it was already under the yoke of the aristocracy.

Nevertheless, even under Polish rule, the memory of the old folkmotes was preserved by the country. Documents of the fifteenth and sixteenth centuries sometimes mention the existence of the veche as of a local assembly with very considerable executive and judicial rights.

Of all the principalities of Russia those of the North-East seem from the most remote times to have been unfavourable to the growth of popular assemblies. In those of Sousdal and of Riasan, the dukes early freed themselves from the necessity of election by the people by establishing primogeniture as the law of succession to the crown. The way in which the eldest son was admitted to succeed to the throne was by associating him, during his father's lifetime, in the exercise of sovereign powers. Vsevolod III. was the first prince who benefited by such a course. He secured the throne to his descendants and thus annulled one of the most important rights of the folkmote, that of choosing the ruler of the land. It is not to be wondered at, therefore, that from the middle of the thirteenth century no mention is made of the popular assemblies of Sousdal.

Up to this point we have tried to show that during the Middle Ages Russia was a loose federation of principalities, in which the people were wont to exercise, on a larger or smaller scale, legislative, executive, judicial, and even political power. By political power I mean the right of electing and dismissing the ruler, of declaring war and making peace. The people exercised their right side by side with the prince, the "knias," who gradually increased his own power to the prejudice of the power of the folkmote or veche. At the end of the fifteenth century Novgorod and Pscov alone maintained the primitive relations between the prince and the popular assembly, for they still kept the power of electing and dismissing the chief magistrate of the state, as well as the highest officials, the posadnik, and the "head of thousands." In the south-western part of Russia the popular assembly became, during the fifteenth and sixteenth centuries, a local administrative, financial, and judicial body, but it lost all political power. In the northern principalities, and especially in Vladimir and Moscow, the folkmotes totally ceased to exist. The growth first of Vladimir and then of Moscow was followed by the complete annihilation of the political rights of the people, and this seems to have been recognised by the writers of the day. Describing the proceedings by which the republic of Novgorod was subjected by the Tzar, Ivan the Third, the chronicle, known under the name of the Patriarch Nikon, says: "In the year 1478 the Tzar declared to the republic "that he wanted Novgorod to be in the exercise of the same power as that which he possessed at Moscow." The inhabitants agreed to comply with his wishes on certain terms, whereby his autocracy would be limited. The Tzar immediately sent the following reply: "I told you that I wanted in Novgorod a state similar to that of Moscow; and instead of that I hear you teaching me how I ought to organise my state in a way different from what it is at present." On hearing this, the citizens sent another embassy to ask what the Tzar meant by saying that he wanted in Novgorod a government like that of Moscow. He answered: "No popular assembly, veche; no elected magistrate, and the whole state in the power of the Tzar."* This answer left no doubt as to his autocratic intentions and their accomplishment in the Moscovite state.

Let us now inquire into the causes which produced this increase of monarchical power. The first seems to have been the great change which had been brought about in the relations between the prince and the popular assembly by the subjection of the prince to the power of the Khans. It is well known that the Tartars, after having established the centre of their European empire on the shores of the Volga, not far from where it joins the Caspian Sea, in the neighbourhood of the modern city of Astrachan, reduced the different principalities of Russia to the condition of vassal states. Leaving the government in the hands of the dynasty of Rurik they forced the Russian princes to receive investiture at the hands of their khans. In such a state of things the prince had no longer any need to trouble himself about his acceptation by the popular assembly of the principality that he intended to govern. In order to secure the throne to himself and his heirs, all that he had to do was to undertake a journey to the southern parts of the Volga and make his appearance at the court of his suzerain—the Khan. Here he had to

* "Complete Collection of Russian Chronicles." vi. 213.

lay out large sums of money in presents and bribes, until at last the Khan was induced to grant a charter, "jarlik," acknowledging the right of the claimant to occupy the throne of his ancestors. From the beginning of the fourteenth century the Moscovite princes had no longer to undertake the journey in person, as the khans had consented to forward the charter of confirmation direct to Moscow on condition that they first received large sums of money from the prince who claimed the throne. The succession was settled at each vacancy by an agreement between the suzerain and the vassal, and the popular assembly had no opportunity of interfering.

Foreign events, especially the rise of the Florentine Union and the capture of Constantinople by the Turks, also largely contributed to the increase of the Moscovite autocracy.

During the period which began with the acceptance of the tenets of the Greek Church by the Russian duke, Vladimir, at the end of the eleventh century, and which ended with the decision of the Byzantine Emperor to subscribe the act of union with the Roman Church, the Russian State as well as the Russian Church remained to a certain extent dependent on the Greek Patriarch and Emperor at Constantinople. In ecclesiastical matters this dependence was manifested in the direct nomination of the Russian Metropolitan by the Byzantine Patriarch, very often not without interference on the part of the Emperor. In secular matters it was rather theoretical than practical. The Russian clergy more than once advised the Grand Duke of Moscovy to recognise the "Tzar of the Greeks" as his lord paramount, and each time they repeated the popular theory that the Byzantine Emperor was the chief of the whole Christian world and therefore the sovereign lord of all Christian kings and potentates. This theory had been first brought forward by Byzantine writers, who actually declared that Constantine the Great had conferred the title of Tabularius on the ruler of Russia as a recompense for his allegiance to the Greek Empire. Up to the end of the fourteenth century the title of "Tzar" was exclusively applied in Russia to the Emperor of Constantinople, and no Russian prince was allowed to dignify himself with it. The Russian clergy, in offering public prayer for the health of the Emperor at Constantinople, spoke of him as of "the Emperor of the Romans and Ruler of the Universe." *

The attitude of Basileus III., Grand Duke of Russia, during the time of the Florentine Union, his bold opposition to the Patriarch Photius and to any compromise with the Romish Church, led the Russian clergy to look upon him and his heirs as the champions of orthodoxy in religion. While the Duke of Moscovy was considered the sole protector of the Greek Church, the Emperor at Constantinople had become, in the eyes of the Russians, a schismatic.

* Compare Diakonov, "The Supreme Power of the Moscovite Tzars," Petersburg, 1889.

It was in order to free Moscovy from all dependence on a schismatic Emperor that the account of the conversion of the Eastern Slavs to Christianity was altered. The apostle St. Andrew, who, according to Armenian and Georgian traditions had been the first to preach the Gospel in the Caucasus, was officially declared to have been the St. John the Baptist of the Russians; Constantinople, being thus deprived of the honour of being the birthplace of Russian Christianity, was accordingly dispossessed of any right to exercise ecclesiastical supremacy over the Russian Church.

The fall of Constantinople, which closely followed the Florentine Union, settled the question of the ecclesiastical autonomy of Russia, and contributed at the same time to strengthen the power of the Moscovite Duke. The Greek Church had lost her secular head in the person of the last Emperor of Constantinople, and the Slavonic principalities of the Balkan Peninsula, as well as the subjugated Greeks, naturally turned their eyes towards the most powerful of the Orthodox rulers. This was the Grand Duke of Moscovy, whose firm allegiance to the ancient creed, and uncompromising attitude towards the Florentine Union, contrasted favourably with the attitude of the last Emperors towards the Popes of Rome. People were led to acknowledge that the fall of Constantinople was a well-deserved punishment on a schismatic ruler, and they were also induced to believe that the conquest of that city by the Turks ought to be the occasion for the transfer of civil supremacy over the Greek Church from Constantinople to Moscovy, from the Emperor to the Grand Duke.

These ideas grew in strength when the last Emperor's sister, Sophia Palæologus, became by marriage the wife and mother of Moscovite princes. A report was spread that the Imperial title had been transferred to the Grand Duke Ivan by no less a person than his wife's brother, the legal heir of the Byzantine Empire. The Grand Duke was anointed with great solemnity, and received the title of "Tzar," a title which, as we have seen, had hitherto been exclusively given to the Greek Emperors. An offer which the German Emperor made through his special envoy, Herbertstein, to grant the title of "king" to the Moscovite Grand Duke on condition of his recognising his dependence upon the Holy Roman Empire, was solemnly rejected; and in order to confirm the new theory of the complete autonomy of the Russian tzardom, a genealogy was invented, showing the direct descent of the house of Rurik from Augustus and his supposed brother Pruss, the mythical founder of Prussia. One fact, however, stood in the way of a universal recognition of these new pretensions to complete autonomy; that was the continued dependence of the Moscovite rulers on the khans of the Tartars. But this was put an end to by Ivan III., who was consequently the first to adorn himself with the title of "Autocrat" (Samoderjez), which to this day continues to be the title of the Russian Tzars.

As Greek monks, and among them the well-known Maxime, began to settle in Russia, Byzantine ideas about the derivation of monarchical power from God, which were already entertained by some of our monkish writers, were rapidly spread among the people. It is not without good reason that the celebrated antagonist of Ivan the Terrible, Prince Kourbsky, accuses the monks of having been the chief source of the servile theory, according to which "the Tzar, in order to preserve his independence, ought to have no counsellors more intelligent than himself." This theory was accepted with avidity by such tyrants as Ivan the Cruel, who refers to it more than once in his correspondence with the Polish king, Stephen Bathory. The fact that this prince was surrounded by a sort of parliament, the Polish Seim, was declared by the Russian Tzar to be a manifest proof of his political inferiority. "Autocracy (samoderjavsto)," according to Ivan's idea, "was impossible with an elective council; the autocrat must do everything by himself; he has to give orders to his subjects, and these last must obey like serfs, and that according to the command of God."

These ideas, which had been expressed centuries before by monkish writers, who had found them set forth in Byzantine treatises, were far from being those of the generality of Russian statesmen and thinkers. When Prince Kourbsky advised the tyrant Ivan to seek good and useful counsel, not only among the members of his *douma,* a sort of *curia regis*—but also among the representatives of the people—*vsenarodnich chelovok*—he gave utterance to an old political desire. Another contemporary writer, the unknown author of *The Sermon of the Saints of Walaam,* gives way to the same feeling in the following terms: "The clergy ought to advise the Tzar to keep a constant general council, composed of persons coming from all the cities and districts of his dominions. Such a council must be kept, and their advice taken day by day on every question which may occur."

Two different institutions were meant by those who advised the Czar to rule by the advice of his councillors. One was as old as the monarchy itself, and belonged to those old customs, which, according to contemporary writers, had been scrupulously maintained by former potentates. I refer to the Council of the Boyars—the Douma. The other institution, the history of which will form the principal subject of our next lecture, was, on the contrary, quite recent—the States-General of Moscovy, the Zemskii Sobor.

I will conclude what I have to say on the political organisation of Russia during that intermediate period which lasted from the fall of the ancient folkmotes to the convocation of the States-General by a description of the first-named council, the Douma.*

* This subject has been very ably discussed by Professor Kluchevsky

The study of the internal constitution of the Douma is indispensable for the comprehension of the part which the higher nobility were called upon to play in the management of the Moscovite State. It will show that the power of the Moscovite princes, absolute as it was, was yet to a certain extent limited by the power of the nobility. Up to the middle of the sixteenth century the Boyars were the only persons admitted to the exercise of executive, military, and judicial authority. Under the name of voevods we find them at the head of provinces, commanding their military forces and managing their administrative interests. As members of the Douma, they had to advise the Tzar on all kinds of political, executive, military, and financial questions. No law was promulgated until after previous deliberation on it by the Douma. The same Douma furnished the chief rulers of the State during the minority of the Tzar, and it was in this way that the power of the Boyars made itself felt among the lower classes of the population, who soon came to look upon them as the chief cause of their misery.

The composition of the Moscovite council was at the beginning very like that which we find in France under the early Capetian kings. The *curia regis* was chiefly formed from among the high court officials, such as the majordome, the marshal, the constable, the chancellor or cancellarius, the camerer or camerarius, etc. The same may be said of the Moscovite Douma of the fourteenth century, as well as of the privy council of each and every of the principalities into which mediæval Russia was divided anterior to the centralising growth of the Moscovite power. The business transacted at the court of a Russian prince being distributed among different departments, the heads of these departments were summoned to sit in the council and received the name of boyars. Money being scarce, the boyars were paid for their services by the donation of crown lands, and this mode of payment being known under the name of "pout," the surname of the boyars was "poutevii boyari." Most of the boyars summoned to sit in the Douma were exempted from military service, and especially from the duty of opposing the enemy at the head of their own retainers, not so much in the open country as in their own castles. Hence the origin of another surname "wedennii boiari" which distinguished the most powerful members of the Russian mediæval nobility. If we inquire into the origin of those admitted to the princely council, we shall see that they belonged to the same class as that which furnished officers to the army and the chiefs of the central and provincial administration. This class is precisely that known to the Anglo-Saxons as Thanes, and to the Merovingian kings under the title of Antrustions. The peculiarity of mediæval Russia consisted in this, that, being divided into a great number of principalities, it left to the knightly class the liberty of freely choosing the prince whom they would like to follow. The Russian knightly class, corresponding to the "ministeriels" of feudal Germany, the so-called "slougili liudi" or "men of service," were authorised by custom to remain in the service of any prince as long as they pleased, and to change from one prince to another according to their own pleasure. Before attaching himself to any prince the "man of service" signed a sort of contract with the political head of the country in which he intended to settle. On taking service, a charter was delivered to the knight in which his duties and rights were precisely stated, and the prince had no right to infringe these conditions. In case of bad treatment, the knight found no difficulty in leaving the prince whom he was serving and in entering into similar relations with some other of the numerous petty potentates, who ruled over mediæval Russia. This right of freely passing from the service of one prince to that of another was clearly recognised by the following sentence in a treaty signed by the prince of Tver with the Grand Duke of Lithuania, Kasimir, as late as the middle of the fifteenth century, 1449; "Our boyars and men of service may freely withdraw from one of us to the other." This document is probably the last recognition of the liberty of removal once enjoyed by the knightly class.

The increasing power of the Grand Duke of Moscovy could not tolerate this survival of federal autonomy. This prince did not object to the liberty of removal as long as it served his own purposes by increasing the number of persons seeking service in the Moscovite army and Moscovite civil service, but as soon as the tyranny of some of the Grand Dukes caused their own knights to withdraw to Poland and Lithuania, severe measures were taken to put a stop to this movement of emigration. The Grand Duke began to confiscate the grants of land ("*pomestie*") of the departing knights, and every time he could lay hands on one of these seceders he was sure to throw him into prison, very often together with his wife and children. The clergy, always on the side of the secular power, more than once likened the behaviour of a seceding knight to the conduct of Judas, and declared it to be not only treason against the State but also a sin in the eyes of God.

Keeping in mind the facts just mentioned, we shall have no difficulty in explaining the concourse of knights and men of the sword in the grand duchy of Moscovy. The territorial extension of the duchy had necessitated the abolition of a great number of small principalities, and persons formerly belonging to the ruling dynasties and united by ties of blood to the Tzar, were anxious to enter his service. In this manner the knightly class began to number in its ranks a whole group of princely families who were the descendants of those potentates whose dominions had been conquered and annexed by Moscow. Before long the number of persons desirous of taking service under the Grand Duke totally excluded the possibility of personal and separate conventions, such as those which settled the mutual rights and duties of prince and knight in the other principalities of Russia. These personal agreements were superseded by a general enactment, which declared that the man of service occupied a higher or lower rank in the political hierarchy according, first, to the dignity of the family to which he belonged, and, secondly, to the number of years his family had been engaged in the Moscovite service.

It was generally acknowledged that a princely family—that is, a family that had once belonged to the number of ruling dynasties, ought to have precedence over all others among untitled nobles. Whoever could show among his ancestors persons in a high official post had the right to refuse any inferior situation, especially in those cases in which a person of a comparatively new family was to be set over him as his superior. This order of precedence was more than once set aside in consequence of the low condition to which this or that wealthy family had been reduced by the loss of its estates. A Russian noble in a miserable state of poverty was as little entitled to occupy a high official position, as was a penniless English duke, or earl, to take his seat in the House of Lords in the fifteenth century, in the reign of Edward IV.

The rules of precedence, constituting what our ancestors of the fifteenth and sixteenth centuries called "*mestnichestvo*," were scrupulously observed both in the army and in the civil service. They also found expression in the constitution of the Council or Douma. The titled nobility, the princely families, as a rule, occupied the highest rank in the hierarchy of the councillors, the rank of "*doumn iboyars,*" or boyars of the Council.

A certain number of the old Moscovite nobility were allowed to retain their original rank, but the rest of the nobles were by degrees lowered to that of persons whose only distinction was to be "the children of ancient boyars." The documents of the time speak of them in precisely these terms, calling them "*boiarski dieti,*" children of the boyars.

The second rank among the members of the Douma was occupied by those known under the name of "*ocolnichii,*" or persons living immediately about the Duke. This rank in the Douma belonged, as a rule, to members of the old Moscovite nobility, as well as to some of the smaller princely families. The Duke had the right to confer on his "*ocolnichy*" the higher title of boyar as a recompense for his services. The rest of the knightly class were either entirely unconnected with the Council or were simply summoned to be present at some of its sittings. They were known under the general name of "noblemen belonging to the Douma," "*dumnii dvoriani,*" and formed the third rank of Councillors.

The fourth or lowest rank in the Council was composed of those members of the knightly class who condescended to hold second-rate posts in the different executive bodies of the duchy, such as the Foreign Office ("*Posolsky prikaz*"), or the board presiding over temporary or life grants of land (*Pomestni prikaz*). These second-rate bureaucrats, known under the name of secretaries, *diaki*, were regularly admitted to the sittings of the Council, where they formed the lowest but by no means the least influential order.

From what has been said it will be seen that autocratic power in Russia had to deal with certain counterpoises and moderating influences in the political constitution of the country even after the fall of the ancient folkmotes. These checks and restraints had their roots in the old political rights exercised by the chiefs of the almost independent principalities which constituted the unorganised federacy of Russian states. Whilst submitting to the power of the Moscovite prince, these once independent chiefs insisted on the recognition of their privilege to be next after the Tzar, the principal ruler of the country. The so-called *mestnichestvo* was, therefore, a sort of unwritten constitution, recognising in each of the members of the higher nobility his distinct right to a place in the machinery of the State. The lower classes alone had no part in the conduct of public affairs. An end was put to this anomalous situation by the convocation of the States-General. The origin of these States-General, or Sobors, and their further development, will form the subject of our next lecture.

# LECTURE V.

## OLD RUSSIAN PARLIAMENTS.

In our last lecture we showed what causes produced the rise of monarchical power in Russia, and tried to prove that, powerful as was the autocracy of the Czars of Moscovy, it was limited by the political rights of the higher nobility. The exercise of these rights was entrusted to the Douma or Council, and similar powers in matters ecclesiastical were vested in a High Commission, often mentioned by the authors of the time under the name of the consecrated Sobor. This body was composed of the Metropolitan, Archbishops, Bishops, Archimandrites or vicars of the bishops, and the heads of the *black clergy*, the abbots or chiefs of monastic congregations.

In the year 1550 these two assemblies of which the one was an almost complete representation of the higher nobility and bureaucracy, and the second of the *higher* clergy, were changed into a more democratic parliament by the addition of representatives of the lower nobility, the regular military force, and the inhabitants of cities and rural districts. We have very little information as to the reason which induced the Government to appeal to these "men of the people," as the members of this assembly were called by contemporary writers. We are totally ignorant of its composition, and of the nature of the business it was called upon to perform. The speech which Ivan the Terrible delivered in its first session is, however, well known. In it he accuses the boyars of the misgovernment which characterised the first years of his reign and throws on them the whole responsibility for the miseries of the people. He acknowledged at the same time the impossibility of redressing old wrongs by *judicial* means and entreated all classes of the people to compound for them by means of compromises. The meaning of this was that all the judges who were accused of illegal decisions, and officials responsible for administrative wrongs, were authorised to treat within a fixed time directly with those who had complained to the Czar of their misrule. So far as appears from later documents the wish of the Czar was complied with by all classes of the people. Vast reforms followed this first essay of representative assemblies; the principle of election, which had formerly prevailed in the organisation of the commune and the lower courts of justice, was reintroduced in the form of elected judges and aldermen (*goubnii starosti* and *zeloval-niki*). It is very probable that those men were convened to the first Russian parliament who had acknowledged the necessity for such reforms, although we have no contemporary documents to establish this fact.

The amount of information we possess about the second Russian parliament, which was summoned in the year 1566 is much greater. We know the number of persons convened to it, the different classes of the people to which they belonged, and the kind of business they had to perform. We may even guess with a certain degree of probability the way in which they exercised their consultative and deliberative functions. In the year 1558 the Russian military forces were engaged in a war with Poland. This war had its rise in the disputes of the Teutonic Knights settled in Livonia, with the growing power of Russia. Losing one after another their chief fortresses, the Order, through their Grand Master Gotthard Kettler, entered into correspondence with the Polish king, Sigismund, and proposed to accept his suzerainty on condition that he should with his army oppose the further encroachments of Russia. This offer was accepted, and Russia had to decide whether she should withdraw from the Livonian strongholds which were already in her power or go to war with Poland. Under these circumstances Ivan the Terrible, before coming to a decision, wished to take the advice not only of the higher clergy, the members of his Douma, and the high officers of State, with the treasurers and secretaries at their head, but also of the lower nobility, the class directly engaged in military service, and those of the third estate, whose business it was to collect the taxes from the urban population.

If we scrutinise the composition of this second Russian Parliament, we are startled by the fact that with the exception of three gentlemen from Toropeczk, six from Louczk, and twenty-two citizens from the city of Smolensk, all its members were persons residing in Moscow. Russian historians have generally explained this anomaly by saying that the Government, having no time to await the arrival of deputies from the provinces, contented itself with consulting such military men as were then present at Moscow, exception being made only as to the inhabitants of some western cities and districts whose interests were directly engaged in the impending war. Such was the case with Smolensk, Louczk, and Toropeczk. If this was so, the Assembly of 1566 would have no right to figure in the list of Russian Parliaments, being nothing but a local Assembly, something like those "états généraux fractionnés," which were known in France during a great part of the fourteenth and fifteenth centuries. But such is not really the case.* The way in which the military class was represented at the Parliament of 1566 finds its explanation in the organisation of the army at that time. It was then composed of five regiments, quartered in different provinces, each regiment con-

* Compare Kluchevsky's recent article, "On the Representative System of the Sobors," in *Russian Thought*, a monthly periodical, published at Moscow, January, 1890.

taining a greater or smaller number of "district hundreds." The hundred was not a numerical, but a local division. As a rule, the headship of every hundred was entrusted, not to a local military man, but to some Moscovite nobleman, residing in the metropolis, but possessing estates in the district to which the hundred belonged. Under the circumstances I have described, the Czar, before going into the new war, was naturally desirous of consulting the men who had the local command of his army, those Moscovite noblemen who were placed at the head of the local hundreds. Their usual place of abode being the metropolis, it is easy to understand why inhabitants of Moscow were almost the only men summoned to attend the Parliament. When the Sobor was convened the army had just returned from its last expedition against Lithuania and all the military chiefs would then be in Moscow. These chiefs, as has been already mentioned, were paid for their services not by a fixed salary, but by donations of land granted for the term of service, which practicially amounted to a life tenure, and were known by the name of *pomestie*.* The quantity of land corresponded to the position held in the ranks of the army. Some received only one hundred and fifty desiatin,† some two hundred and twenty-five, some even three hundred, and these differences led to the division of the military classes into three groups called *statii*.

* They were much the same as the Carlovingian benefices.

† A *desiatin* is approximately three English acres.

The Sobor of 1566 contained ninety-seven members from the first class and ninety-nine of the second; among the lower group we find only thirty-five from Toropeczk and six from Louzck.

As to the third estate, it was represented by seventy-five men, all belonging to the Moscovite trading class. The reason of this must be sought in the contemporary organisation of the Russian bourgeoisie. During the second part of the sixteenth century we find in Moscow two different classes of tradesmen: one known under the name of "hosts" (*gosti*), the other under that of "merchants" (*koupzi*).

Both classes contained in their ranks not only Moscovite tradesmen, but also tradesmen from other cities. The wealthy and influential merchants of the whole empire were inscribed in the list of the "hosts," the rest composed that of the "merchants." This latter class was sub-divided into Moscovite and Smolensk merchants, the latter being those, whose commerce was chiefly confined to the western provinces of Russia and its natural head Smolensk. In the sixteenth century these same sub-divisions re-appear under somewhat different names, the one being called the hundred of "hosts" (*gostinnaia sotnia*) and the other the hundred of "drapers" (*soukonnaia sotnia*). The divisions I have mentioned were the work of the central government, which regarded the wealthier merchants as its direct helpers in the difficult task of collecting customs and excise duties.

No person belonging to the Guild of "hosts" could refuse to perform these heavy and responsible duties. The man, on whom the choice of his companions fell, was obliged to remove to the city whose taxes he had to collect. So that the exercise of such functions might be entrusted to persons of great local influence, the election fell, as a rule, on a merchant possessing estates or large stocks of merchandise in the city which he was called to administer. Like the guild of hosts, the guilds of Moscovite and Smolensk merchants were called upon to assist the Government in the exercise of its financial authority and accordingly elected among themselves the officers of the excise and customs administration of the smaller urban districts.

It is easy to understand that before engaging in a new war, which would necessarily cause new and heavy expenses, the Czar would desire to obtain information as to the pecuniary resources of the country from those persons whose duty it would be to collect the taxes. He, therefore, summoned to the Sobor the tradesmen of the Guild of hosts and also the Moscovite and Smolensk merchants, or, in other words, all those who had the charge of collecting the revenues of indirect taxation, not only in the metropolis, but throughout the empire. Composed as it was of the high officials, the members of the council, the archbishops, bishops, archimandrites, abbots, and the local heads of the military and financial administration, the Sobor of 1566 was not so much the representative of the people as of the governing class. It is, therefore, difficult to speak of its analogy with the representative assemblies of Western Europe, though some of the elements of which it was composed, are to be found both in the Swedish and the German parliaments. In Sweden the army was called upon to send its generals, colonels, and even its majors to the sittings, at least from 1598 to 1778.* In the German Landestände, as well as in the Swedish States-General, the cities were regularly represented by their officers, the Rathmänner, members of the city council, or Rätta borgare, as they were called in Sweden, just as the French cities and boroughs were usually represented in the Etats Généraux, not by elected deputies, but by their *maires*, *échevins* and *consuls*.†

Now that we are acquainted with the manner in which the first Sobor, this real assembly of notables, was composed, let us take a look at its proceedings. The question on which the Czar wanted advice was whether he should engage in a new war with Poland, or whether it would be better for him to restore to Kasimir the cities which he had conquered in Lithuania. Each estate had to give a separate answer. The clergy declared itself in favour of war. They maintained that Livonia had always belonged

---

* Nordenflicht, "Die Schwedische Staatsverfassung in ihrer geschichtlichen Entwickelung," p. 23.

† Bavelier, "Essai Historique sur le Droit d'Election et sur les Anciennes Assemblées Représentatives en France," p. 92.

to Russia, a preposterous claim which was plainly contradicted by history. Whilst insisting on the impossibility of concluding peace on the terms proposed by Kasimir, they declared themselves incapable of judging what means the Government ought to take for the safety of its new conquests. "The Czar alone must decide the matter. It is not our business to advise him on such questions, but to pray God for the success of his undertakings." This plainly meant that they feared a new imposition of subsidies, and had no desire to take on themselves the initiative of this taxation.

The boyars gave a similar answer. "It is impossible," said they, "to leave in the hands of the Polish king the newly conquered German cities, for in that case the important Russian fortress of Polozk situated on the Dvina, would remain surrounded by the lands of the enemy." They also declared themselves ready to serve the Czar whatever might be his decision. "God alone and the Czar," such was their conclusion, "ought to have the last word in this matter." Some dissentient members of the Douma presented their own opinion in writing. The noblemen of the first and second class or *statii*, also expressed their opinions in two different papers and were unanimous in their desire to retain the Livonian cities. Those of Toropeczk and Louczk, who were more directly concerned in the matter, declared that they would sacrifice their lives for a single "dessiatine" of the cities surrounding Polozk which were claimed by the Polish king. The hosts and merchants of Moscow and Smolensk were not less patriotic in their sentiments, the latter particularly insisting on the impossibility of leaving Polozk without a territorial district attached to it. "A village cannot exist without its own district and still less a fortress," said they. "If the king of Poland gets the territory of Polozk that city will be of no use to the Russians, and nothing will prevent the king building a new fortress just opposite the Russian fortress."

The general result of the conference was that the Czar decided on war.

We find no other General Assembly in the reign of Ivan the Terrible, but we must not infer from that fact that the Czar altogether forbore to apply to the people. On two different occasions we find him addressing the mob of Moscow, once in 1564, in order to get their approval of the prosecution of the boyars for their supposed treason against the State and open plundering of the people; and a second time to ascertain their feelings on the occasion of a fresh discomfiture of the Russian troops by the Poles and the loss, not only of Livonia, but of Polozk and Smolensk. This last convention was in the year 1597 and was the occasion of a long and patriotic speech delivered, in the name of the Czar, by his secretary Schelkalov. This speech, which announced the loss of thousands of Russian soldiers, produced a great impression, chiefly on the women, who, fearing their husbands were dead, went crying through the streets and asking for new ones. Whereupon the secretary made a second speech in which he threatened to have them flogged if they did not cease their lamentations. We thus find the experiment of admitting the people to the discussion of public affairs degenerating, either into appeals to the Moscow mob to sanction, by its consent, acts of cruelty towards the members of the higher nobility, or into threats of flogging made to poor weeping women in their bereavement.

It is difficult to discover in the facts which I have just related any resemblance to a regular consultation of the people in Parliament assembled. The meetings are more like a parody of the ancient folkmotes, the *veche*.

The representative system remained unknown to Russia throughout the sixteenth century. The Assembly which in 1584 confirmed the right of the eldest son of Ivan, Theodor, to occupy the Russian throne, although called "a parliament" by the English Resident Hoarsay, was, according to the same author, composed of nothing but the chief clergy and members of the higher and lower nobility. Another assembly, that of 1585, called to deliberate on the question of clerical immunities and the necessity for subjecting the lands of monasteries to general taxation, contained in its ranks only the higher clergy, the chief officers of the State, and the members of the Council or Douma.

The Rurik family became extinct on the death of

the Czar Theodor, and a new dynasty had to be chosen. The higher nobility seized this opportunity to impose certain limitations on the exercise of the Sovereign power. But the nearest candidate to the throne, Boris Godounov, not being willing to consent to such limitations, refused to accept the throne offered him by the boyars and insisted on the necessity of summoning the cities to decide who should occupy the throne of the Rurik family. He did this in the expectation that the people would oppose any measure limiting the principle of autocracy. The Sobor, which was called together according to his wish, was widely different from the ideal of a truly National Assembly. Of the 457 members who were present at its sittings, 83 belonged to the higher clergy, and 338 to the bureaucracy and the higher and lower nobility. As to the third estate, it was composed of only 21 hosts, of the head of the Guild of hosts and of 13 deputies from the rural districts. This assembly was presided over by the Patriarch, the Chief of the Russian clergy, and unanimously expressed itself favourable to Boris Godounov, to whom the Russian throne was offered unconditionally.

Representatives of the lower classes of the city of Moscow appeared in 1605 at the Sobor to which the false Demetrius entrusted the right of judging the boyar and future Czar, Basilius Schouisky, on account of a rebellion which he had instigated. The Sobor condemned Schouisky to death, but the Czar Demetrius commuted this punishment to perpetual banishment to the City of Viatka, whence he soon returned at the gracious order of the monarch.

The Assembly which in 1606, after the death of the false Demetrius, elected Schouisky as the Czar of Russia, was not a Sobor in the true sense of the word, for it was chiefly composed of the boyars. The Moscow mob nevertheless sanctioned the election, and the new Czar was eagerly proclaimed at the so-called "read place," in front of the palace.

This election of Schouisky has some claim to our attention, as it was the first at which constitutional limits were imposed on Russian autocracy. The newly elected Czar had no immediate relation with the dynasty of Rurik, and was but the equal of the other boyars. He was known to be vindictive and to have a great number of relations and friends who would be ready enough to make use of his power for their own advantage. All this induced the boyars to protect their own interests by the creation of rules which their nominee was obliged to accept. According to Strahlenberg, the well-known author of the "Historical and Geographical Description of the Northern and Eastern parts of Europe and Asia" (a book written in German and published at Stockholm in the year 1703), the constitutional limitations imposed were as follows: "No new law was to be made and no innovations were to be introduced in the old legislation without the consent of the Douma. (Strahlenberg calls it senatus.) No new contributions were to be levied unless previously discussed and accepted by the same Council."* These constitutional limitations as you may easily perceive, were exactly the same as those established in England by the Magna Charta and the statute of Edward the First, *de tallagio non concedendo,* but whilst the English people entrusted the care of their liberty to the lords, gentlemen, and citizens in Parliament assembled, the Russian boyars wanted to keep to themselves the exclusive control of the sovereign power. This caused the failure of their constitution, and was the chief reason why, on the occasion of a new election, the control of the Constitutional compromise entered into by the people and the Czar, was no longer entrusted to the Douma of the boyars, but to the representative Assembly of the whole nation—that is to the Sobor.

Schouisky reigned only a few years. In 1610 he lost the crown by the decision of a new Assembly which assumed the title of Zemski Sobor, although it was chiefly composed of the boyars and the Moscow mob. This took place in the middle of July. A month later a treaty was signed by the boyars and the chief of the Polish army, by which Vladislas, son of Sigismund, king of Poland, was called to the throne of Russia. Like his predecessor, the new Czar accepted certain constitutional limitations, amongst others that of administering justice according to the

* "Historisch-Geographische Beschreibung der Nördl. und Oestl. Theile von Europa und Asien," p. 202.

existing customs and the rules by law established. No alterations in the latter could be made, except with the consent of the Council (Douma) of "the whole land." These last words meant the Zemski Sobor, the States-General or Parliament of Russia.

I shall not attempt to narrate the events which prevented the accession of a Polish and Catholic prince to the throne of Russia. It will be enough for my purpose to state that the people and the clergy were unanimous in their dislike to this foreign and "heretical" ruler. The folkmotes, or *veches*, not only in Novgorod, but also in those parts where they had hitherto been quite unknown, as in Kasan, or Nijni Novgorod, entered into correspondence with each other, local militia united, and an army, called into existence by the patriotic sentiments of simple burgesses like Minin, marched from Nijni Novgorod to Moscow, under the command of Pojarsky. At the same time a correspondence was begun with the object of forming a new Sobor, which was to be a really representative body, composed of delegates sent by all the estates. The writs of summons sent out by the head of the army, Pojarsky, have fortunately been preserved, so that we can get a clear notion of what was meant at that time by the term "General Council of the land," a term employed more than once in the documents of the time. Addressing the people of Poutivl or of Wichegodsk, the commander-in-chief insists on the necessity of sending to Jaroslav, the place selected for the meeting of the new Assembly, two or three men from each of the estates (*chinov*) of the nation. From Jaroslav the Sobor, following the army, removed to Moscow, where it sat in common with the boyars of the council, the high commission of the clergy (*osviaschenni Sobor*), and the representatives of the regular and irregular military forces, that is, the Strelzi and the Cossacks. It was this Assembly which elected Michael Theodorovich Romanov to be Czar of Russia.

Before proceeding to the election of the Czar, the Sobor called on all the inhabitants of the country to fast for three consecutive days. It then passed a law, due mainly to the influence of the popular section of the Assembly, prohibiting the election of any foreign prince. The nobility would have had no objection to the placing of a Swedish or Polish pretender on the vacant throne. The higher and lower orders differed widely as to the man they wished to choose from among the Russian boyars; the names of Golitzin, Vorotinsky, Troubezkoy, and even that of the dethroned Basilius Schouisky, were, for a time, to be found on the list of candidates supported by the nobility. The first to declare himself in favour of the young Romanov was one of his relations named Scheremetiev, and his proposal was favourably listened to by the lower nobility, the Cossacks and the burgesses. His election, however, was so unexpected an event that his own father, a bishop then closely imprisoned by the Poles, was the first to suggest, in a letter written to Scheremetiev, that certain constitutional limits should be imposed on the power of the future Czar. Strahlenberg* is quite correct in his statement that the idea of these limitations was borrowed from Poland where already in the middle of the sixteenth century, under Stephen Bathory, the States-General, or Seim, and the Council possessed considerable rights. The reasons which operated in favour of the young Michael Romanov were, first of all, his relationship with the extinct dynasty of Rurik through his great aunt, Anastasia Romanov, who was one of the wives of Ivan the Terrible; secondly, the small number of relations which was looked upon as a safeguard against further depredations on the demesne lands in the form of beneficiary donations; and thirdly, the popularity of his family, which had been persecuted by the boyars from the time of Boris Godounov. His father, Philarete, who had been forced to become a monk, was especially endeared to the nation by his virtues; he had attained a high position among the clergy, having been made Bishop of Jaroslav.

The late Patriarch Germogen, who had been much beloved by the people, had also been favourably disposed towards the election of young Romanov, and this fact contributed greatly to secure him the sympathy of the clergy. At the time of his election Michael was but a boy of fifteen, and his father being a prisoner in Magdeburgh, Scheremetiev and the

* P 284.

members of his party looked upon it as highly probable that the real government would pass into their hands.

The Sovereign power which was offered to young Romanov was far from being the same as that enjoyed by Ivan the Terrible. Autocratic power had had to yield before the new theories of constitutional limitations directly imported from Poland. That Michael had to sign a compromise is a fact briefly mentioned by Russian eye-witnesses, such as Kotoschichin, as well as by foreigners then residing in Russia. The chronicles of the city of Pskov speak of it in contemptuous terms. It was not enough, say they, for the boyars to have reduced the country to the miserable state to which they had brought it. They wanted to go on in the same way of pillage and oppression; they had no regard for the Czar, did not fear him on account of his youth, and all the more so since they had induced him, at the time of his accession to the throne, to take an oath, by which he renounced the right of inflicting capital punishment on persons belonging to the higher nobility. Capital punishment was to be superseded by close imprisonment. No mention is made in the chronicles of any further limitation of the Sovereign power of the Czar.

The well-known Kotoschichin, who was alive at the time, speaking of the accession of the Czar Alexis, son of Michael Romanov, notices the fact that, "contrary to the custom established by his predecessor, the new Czar signed no charter by which he undertook to inflict capital punishment only in accordance with law and justice, and to consult the boyars and men of the Douma on each and every question concerning the government of the land, so that no decision might be come to without their assent."

Although Kotoschichin speaks more positively as to the constitutional character of the limitations imposed on Russian autocracy in the first quarter of the seventeenth century, we must notice the fact that he says nothing of the part which the Sobor or Parliament was called upon to play in this experiment in limited monarchy. He mentions only the boyars and the men of the Douma, not "those of the land," a phrase used at that time when speaking of the members of the Zemski Sobor.

The Swedish writer, Fokkerodt, is more explicit when he affirms that in the compromise signed by Michael, the young Czar promised to give free course to the judicial proceedings of the courts, so as to inflict no punishment on his own authority, to introduce no new law without the consent of the Sobor, to abstain from levying any tax without the consent of this representative Assembly, and to begin no war without its counsel and approbation.

As to Strahlenberg, his statement is as follows: Before the coronation Michael was forced to accept the following conditions: He promised to (1) uphold and protect the existing creed of Russia; (2) to keep no memory of injuries inflicted on his family, to forget and to forgive all past animosities; (3) He took also the obligation to make no new laws or alter old ones, and to take no important measure which might contradict the existing laws, or suspend the legal proceedings of the courts of justice; (4) He promised as well to begin no wars and to make no peace by his own will.*

This view of the power of the Sobor is confirmed by the fact of its quasi-permanent presence at Moscow during the whole reign of the first Romanov. The laws and proclamations issued at that time generally contain the following characteristic expression: "According to our order (*oukas*) and the decision of the whole land (*po vsei zemli prigovorou*)." The whole land cannot mean anything else than the representatives in Parliament assembled.

Many important questions were discussed and settled by the Sobor. In the first years of the reign want of money obliged the Czar more than once to have recourse to forced loans and benevolences.

---

* "Vor dem Crönungs Act hat Michael folgende Puncte und conditiones acceptirt und unterschrieben, nähmlich: (1) Die Religion zu erhalten und zu schützen; (2) alles was seinem Vater widerfahren zu vergessen und zu vergeben, und keine particulare Feindschaft, sie möge Nahmen haben wie sie wolle zu gedenken; (3) keine neue Gesetze zu machen, oder alte zu ändern, hohe und wichtige Sachen nach dem Gesetze und nicht allein vor sich selbst, sondern durch ordentlichen Procez urtheilen zu lassen; (4) weder Krieg noch Frieden allein und vor sich selbst mit dem Nachbar vorzunehmen und; (5) seine Güter zur Bezeugung der Gerechtigkeit und Vermeidung aller Procesz mit particularen Leuten, entweder an seine Familie abzutreten oder solche denen Kron-Güthern einzuverleiben" (p. 209).

These were levied side by side with the regular taxes on the goods of merchants and peasants (*torgovii i soschnii liudi*); the taxes received the consent of the Sobor, the benevolences were endorsed by it. The nomination of a new Patriarch in 1619 was also their work. The annals of the time tell us that the boyars, the dignitaries of the Court, and all the people of the "Moscovite State" called on Michael and asked him to induce his father Philarete to accept the primacy of the Russian church. Two years later, in 1621, a new Sobor was consulted on the question as to whether Russia should go to war with Poland. The Estates gave an answer in the affirmative, but the want of money and soldiers forced the Government to postpone the execution of this decision.

From 1622 the Sobors lose their character of quasi-constant assemblies, each remaining in session for several years, and begin to be called only on special occasions, whenever their services were required for the settlement of important questions of State.

In 1632 war with Poland necessitated the levying of new subsidies. The Sobor was accordingly assembled and gave its consent to the imposition of a general tax on all the estates of the empire, on the tradesmen as on the "men of service." The amount of money to be demanded from the latter was not fixed; each person could pay what he liked. The sums produced by the tax were intended for the payment of the army. During the next two years we find the Sobor consulting the Czar on matters of war and taxation, on the relations of the land with Poland and the Tartars of the Crimea. The Czar complained of the ill-treatment to which his envoy was subjected by the Khan. The superior clergy, whose answer alone has been preserved, insisted on the necessity of building fortresses on the Southern boundaries of the Moscovite empire, in those cities of the Ukraine, which like Belgorod or Voroneg, remained for centuries the pioneers of Christianity and culture in the southern steppes of Russia, and which were periodically plundered by the Tartars.

Two years later the military occupation of Asov by the Cossacks of the Don and the impending necessity of a war with the Crimean Tartars for the preservation of the conquest, caused a new Sobor to be convened. This Assembly was in favour of war and accordingly ordered the levy of military forces, "even from the villages belonging to the crown land and the lands of the clergy."

In 1642 matters concerning the fortress of Asov again became the immediate cause of a new assembling of the Russian Estates. As the Turks had no intention of leaving Asov in the hands of the Cossacks, who were not able to hold it themselves, the question of annexing it to the Russian state suggested itself to the Government, though it involved the risk of incurring the responsibility of a new and almost imminent war. The Czar finding it necessary to know the feeling of the nation, summoned one hundred and ninety-five persons elected by the Estates, besides the Douma or Privy Council. and the superior clergy, to Moscow. Nearly all classes of society sent representatives, each class gave its opinion or advice separately on papers bearing the signatures of all the members of the same Estate, while the dissentients sent in their opinions on separate and private papers.

The superior clergy, faithful to their old habits, assured the Czar that they were quite unable to advise him on the question; it was not, they said, their custom to do so, for it was the business of the Czar and his Douma; their sole duty was to invoke God's blessing on the Czar's undertakings. Should the Czar, however, want military aid, they declared themselves ready to make the necessary sacrifices in order to pay the soldiers, and that according to their means. The majority of the Moscovite nobility expressed themselves in favour of annexation. The Czar ought to hold the newly acquired fortress, but he should merely order the Cossacks to continue their occupation of it. Volunteers alone ought to be necessary to give help and assistance. Some advised that soldiers should be sent to Asov, not only from the cities of the Ukraine, but even from Moscow. All sorts of men, with the exception of serfs and such as had lost their liberty through not having paid their debts, ought to be selected for that purpose. If money were wanted, each Estate ought to nominate two or three persons whom the Czar might authorise to levy subsidies from all persons and goods, from officers (*prikasnii*) and the Czar's suite, from widows and orphans, from "hosts" and merchants, and from each and every person not engaged in military service.

Some of the nobility, amongst others those of Vladimir, simply promised to obey the Czar's orders, pointing at the same time to the miserable state of their cities and country, which they said was well-known to the Czar and to the boyars of his Douma. Much more peremptory was the advice given by the local nobility of certain larger cities, such as Sousdal, Juriev (the modern Dorpat), Novgorod, and Rostov. They were of opinion that the surrender of Asov would bring down the wrath of God: "The Czar cannot leave in the hands of the infidels," said they, "the holy images of John the Baptist and of St. Nicholas." If the army wanted victuals they might be taken out of the magazines belonging to the cities of the Ukraine. Military aid could be given from Moscow and the expenses for the victualling of the army ought to be laid upon the whole land, without exception. Complaining of the great quantity of land given in benefices to the boyars and of the large amount of money got by bribes and extortions by the officers of the State (*prikasnii*), who afterwards invested it in vast buildings and palaces, the burgesses insisted on the necessity of laying part of the burden of the future war on the shoulders of that class, and of obliging them to arm the soldiers; they maintained, moreover, that their fortunes should be taxed like those of all other classes of the State. The same measures ought also to be taken with the clergy, the bishops and abbots being equally called on to equip warriors, according to the number of serfs they possessed. The Czar ought to issue an ukase, stating the number of serfs a soldier ought to possess, or rather the proportion existing between the number of his serfs and the service required of him. This proportion should be strictly maintained in future, and those who had not serfs enough ought to receive new gifts of serfs from the government. Money for purposes of war, they also insisted, might be taken out of the treasuries of the Patriarch and the monasteries.

The lower nobility, or what is the same thing, the men-of-war of the cities of Toula, Kolomna, Serpouchov, Riazan, Kalouga, &c., were even more precise in their demands that the proportion of military service should tally with the number of serfs which each man-of-war or knight possessed. Those who had over fifty serfs ought to serve without pay, and also contribute to the expenses of the war by supplying food to the army, whilst those who had not more than fifty ought to be free from the latter obligation.

If we turn our attention to the "written opinions" given in by the members of the third estate, we find them complaining of the miserable state into which they had recently fallen, partly because all the commerce of Moscow was in the hands of foreigners, and partly because of the oppression of the *voivodes,* or

Governors of provinces, who had superseded the freely-elected heads of districts (the *goubnii starosti* of the sixteenth century). The delegates of the hosts and merchants of Moscow nevertheless insist on the necessity of holding Asov, pointing out at the same time that they receive no lands from the Crown, and have more trouble than profit in the levying of taxes and excise duties, and generally suggesting to the Czar the impossibility of increasing their payments.

The "memorial" of the hundredmen and headmen of the black hundreds and townships, under which name must be understood the representatives of the rural population, contains more or less the same complaints and similar desires. The people are exhausted by taxes, forced labour, military service, &c.; they have also suffered much from fire; the *voivodes* have ruined them by their exactions; so miserable is their condition that many of them have run away, leaving their houses and lands. The conclusion of this very interesting document has unfortunately not come down to us.

Our general impression on reading the memorials or petitions of this Sobor is that, although all Estates were unanimous in their patriotic desire to keep their hold on the newly conquered fortress, they still felt themselves scarcely in a position to bear the expense of a new war with the Turks; and sharing in these apprehensions the Czar did not dare to incur the responsibility, and sent orders to the Cossacks to withdraw from Asov.

The Sobor of 1642 was the last general Assembly convened by the first of the Romanovs.

Although the direct successor of Michael, Alexis Michaelovich, ascended the throne without entering into any covenant with his people, nevertheless the Sobor was called to confirm the act of his coronation. This happened in 1645. Four years later the Sobor was called upon to aid in the important business of codification. Modern inquirers have brought to light the fact that the petitions presented at this Assembly more than once furnished important materials for the reformation of the Russian law, and that their influence may be traced through the whole code of Alexis (known under the title of *Oulogenie*). During the following year the Sobor was again convened at Moscow in order to advise the Government as to the suppression of insurrectionary movements in different parts of the empire, and especially at Pskov. The Assembly advised lenient treatment of the insurgents, and the Government acted accordingly.

In 1651 and 1653 the Sobor on two different occasions declared itself in favour of the annexation of Little Russia. This country had been liberated from the Poles by the "Hetman" of the Cossacks, Bogdan Chmelnizky, who soon afterwards offered it to the Czar of Russia. It was feared that the acceptance of this offer might involve Russia in a new war with Poland; therefore the advice of the Sobor of 1651 was only conditional. If Poland acquiesced in the demands of the Czar, Russia was to abstain from annexation; if not, the risk of a new war ought not to be avoided, and Christian brethren were to be taken under the protection of the orthodox Czar. Three years later, when the Polish king Jan Kasimir entered into direct alliance with the ancient enemies of Russia—the Swedes and the Crimean Tartars—and when therefore no doubt could be entertained as to the necessity for war, the Sobor openly invited the Czar to take the Hetman and the Cossacks of the Dnieper "under his high hand, together with their cities and lands, and that in order to preserve the true Orthodox Church." The delegates spoke of their readiness to fight the Polish king and to lose their lives for the honour of the Czar.

The Sobor of 1653 was the last general Assembly called in the time of Alexis. Following the example of his predecessors, the Czar on several occasions also convened representatives of one single estate to consult with them on matters directly concerning their order. Such an assembly of notables sat in Moscow in the year 1617. It consisted chiefly of Moscovite merchants. It was convened to hear the opinion of Russian tradesmen as to the desirability of granting to English merchants trading in Moscow, and to their chief agent, John Merrick, the right of making explorations in search of a new road to China and India "by way of the river Ob." The majority of the delegates were opposed to the project.

The same feeling of animosity towards foreigners found its expression in 1626, when on the demand of English merchants to be allowed to trade with Persia, the members of the guild of guests and the Moscow merchants insisted on the necessity of upholding the monopoly which the Moscovite tradesmen enjoyed in going to Astrachan to buy Persian goods. The majority of the merchants declared themselves unable to compete with foreign merchants, and even the minority were of opinion that if free trade were permitted to English traders in return for large payments made by them to the crown, this liberty ought not to be extended to the traffic in Russian commodities. Half a century later, in 1667, the same Moscovite merchants, consulted by Alexis, stoutly opposed the demand of Armenian merchants for free trade in Persian commodities, and begged the Government not to endanger their own trade by foreign competition. Ten years later the Moscow tradesmen, together with the delegates of the black hundreds and villages, were called together to give their opinion as to the causes which tended to raise the price of corn. They complained of engrossers and asked that their practices might be forbidden in future. They also spoke of the great damage agriculture had sustained through recent wars. The increase in the number of distilleries was also mentioned as one of the principal reasons for the dearness of corn.

In 1681–2 the "men of service" were convened together with the Douma to reform the military administration. It was this memorable Assembly which abolished the old custom of appointing men to the chief posts in the army, not according to their personal merit, but to the rank of their family, and the length of time it had served the State; and which also ordered the heraldic books to be burnt.

The last instances we have of the convening of the Russian Sobors belong to the period of internal trouble which followed the death of the Czar Theodore. In 1682 a Sobor to which the inhabitants of Moscow alone were summoned, pronounced itself in favour of the occupation of the vacant throne by the youngest son of Alexis, the future emperor, Peter the Great. A new Assembly, which in its composition answered even less than its predecessor to the idea of a general representative council, was convoked a few months later by the party that favoured the political designs of the Princess Sophia, sister to Peter the Great. It insisted on the division of the sovereign power between the two brothers of Theodore, Peter and John. Princess Sophia became from that time the real ruler of the empire. Again Moscow alone was represented though the Acts speak of the presence of delegates from all the provinces and cities of the empire.

It was in 1698 that the Sobor was convoked for the last time. It was called together to pronounce judgment on the Princess Sophia who, during the absence of Peter the Great in the Western States of Europe, had tried by the help of the *strelzi* (a kind of Life-Guards) to seat herself on the Russian throne.

The only contemporary writer who mentions this Assembly is a German of the name of Korb, who was secretary of the German Legation. According to him the young monarch insisted on this occasion on the presence of two delegates from each of the Estates, beginning with the highest and ending with the lowest. Unfortunately no information has come down to us as to the decision arrived at by this quasi-general representative body of the Russian people.

One fact especially merits our attention: The Sobors were never abolished by law. They simply ceased to exist just as did the States-General of France from the beginning of the seventeenth (1613) to the end of the eighteenth century. No legal act, therefore, lies in the way of a new convocation of the representatives of the empire. Should the present Emperor convoke them, in so doing he would be in perfect accord with the first founders of his dynasty, and also with the promises contained in the Magna Charta of the first Romanov.

Turning from the political history of the old Russian Parliaments, we will now consider their internal constitution. As we have seen, the seventeenth century introduced a complete change in their composition. During the reign of Ivan the Terrible the administrative and military classes had alone been represented; from the time of the interregnum they became meetings of delegates from all the different Estates. The following were the classes of the people who were represented: the superior clergy, the higher nobility, the lower clergy, and the lower nobility, or what is the same thing the ministerial or knightly class as they were called at that time, the three Guilds of Moscovite merchants, the citizens of the different urban districts and, on two different occasions, in 1614 and 1682, the black hundreds and villages, which meant in the technical language of the time, the peasants established on the lands of the State. Serfs, and persons who had lost their personal liberty on account of debts or any other reason, were never admitted to the right of representation. The army was very often represented by delegates from the regular regiments, such as the *strelzi*, and some irregular troops, the Cossacks for instance. The large extent of the Russian dominions and the consequent remoteness of certain places from the metropolis, was a natural barrier to the appearance of certain delegates at the Sobor. It was for this reason that the cities of Siberia remained without representation. Other places less remote got exemption from the duty of choosing delegates on account of the bad state of the roads and the difficulty and even danger connected with travelling. Some few considered it a great burden, on account of the expense of the journey and the maintenance of the delegates. In this they acted like those mediæval English cities and boroughs, which under the Plantagenets did their best to shirk the duty of representation. The number of persons sent by each electoral circuit was not strictly fixed. Generally the writs of summons speak of two or three delegates.

The electoral district was, as a rule, the city and its outlying parts. Larger cities, as Novgorod, constituted by themselves several districts; in Novgorod there were no less than five such districts. The Metropolis (Moscow) was largely represented by delegates from the lower nobility, by those of the three classes of Moscovite traders and the representatives of the black hundreds and villages.

The writs of summons were addressed to the *voivodes,* or Governors of provinces, and to the *goubnii starosti,* or elective district heads.

To give you a clear notion of the mode in which the elections were managed, I will translate one of these writs. The writ in question was issued on the 9th of September, 7128, counting from the beginning of the world (that is the year 1619): "In the name of the Czar Michael, the *voivode* of Oustujna, named Boutourlin, is ordered to elect among the clergy, one man or two, and from the nobility (the sons of boyars) two persons, and two more from the inhabitants of the urban district (*posadskii liudi*). The persons must be well-to-do and intelligent, capable of narrating the wrongs they have sustained, and the oppression and destruction which they have suffered. The election rolls must be sent by the *voivode* to Moscow, and should be received not later than on St. Nicholas's day."

The *voivode*, or *goubnoi starosta*, as soon, as the writ was in his hands, summoned the electors and ordered them to proceed to the nomination of their delegates. Each estate or order acted separately. In answer to the writs they had received, the *voivodes* sent in a detailed account of the election proceedings. Several of these very interesting documents have been found in the archives of the Ministry of Justice in Moscow. Professor Latkin has published a great many of them in his valuable "Materials for a History of the Sobors," and, in reading them, the conclusion is arrived at, that the election as a rule was made by the Estates themselves, without the intervention of the *voivode* or *oubnoi storasta*. "The nobility of Voroneg," states the *voivode* of this place, Prince Alexis Krapotkin, in the year 1651, "have elected from among themselves two persons, the one called Trofim Michnev, and the other Theodor Philoppof. The citizens only one person named Sacharof, and I, your Majesty's slave (*cholop*), have sent you these three men to Moscow." The action of those *voivodes*, who, instead of consulting the electors, proceeded to a direct nomination of the delegates, was sometimes disavowed. Such was, for instance, the case of the *voivode* of Kropivna, a certain Astafiev. In the letters sent to him in the name of the Government, he was greatly blamed for having misunderstood the orders given to him, "the nobility were asked to elect a good nobleman from among themselves, and you had no justification for making the nomination of the delegate yourself."

The delegate belonged, as a rule, to the same estate as his elector, but it sometimes happened that on account of the small number of persons capable of supporting the burden of representation, a person of another order was intrusted with the duty of delegate. The *voivodes* and *starostas* mention more than once such facts as the following. In 1651 the *starosta* of Zvenigorod, Elizar Marcov, declares in a letter addressed to the Czar, that it was impossible for him to nominate a delegate from among the inhabitants of the city district (*posadskii liudi*), for the best of them were engaged in masonry work at the Storojevoy monastery, accomplishing their "hedge duty," which they owed to the crown (*ogradnaia povinnost*). Another *starosta* from Kropivna wrote at the same time, that in his district the number of city residents was not more than three. They were all very poor and gained their livelihood by going from one household to another to work at cleaning the court-yards. Therefore, he found it more suitable to name a gentleman to represent them at the Sobor.

The delegates, as a rule, received instructions called *Nakasi*, in which the electors stated their opinions on the chief subjects to be discussed at the General Assembly. Unfortunately no documents of this kind have been preserved, and we know of their existence only through their being by chance mentioned in some contemporary documents. Speaking of the delegates summoned to the Sobor of 1613, the charters of the time directly state, that they brought with them from Moscow "complete instructions" (*dogovori*) concerning the election of the Czar. The delegates received from their electors the supply of victuals (*zapassi*), which they would need during their stay in Moscow. Nevertheless they very often made an application to the Government for money to cover their expenses. This fact is mentioned more than once in the documents of the time. The writs of summons establish no rule as to the amount of fortune which a delegate was required to possess; they only recommend the election of "good sensible, and wealthy persons, accustomed to treat of matters of State." This did not imply that the delegates were required to know the rules of grammar or to be able to sign their names on the rolls of the Sobor correctly. The number of illiterate persons was rather large even at so late an Assembly as that of 1649, and they were to be found, not only among the lower nobility and the representatives of cities, but also in the ranks of the boyars; not, however, in those of the higher clergy.

The ordinary place of meeting was the palace in the Hall called the *granovitaia Palata.* Sometimes the Sobor sat in the palace of the Patriarch, or in the Cathedral (*Ouspenski Sobor*). The session was opened either by the Czar in person, or, as was more often the case, by one of his secretaries, who, in a written paper or in a speech, declared the reason for which the Assembly was called together, and the questions it had to discuss. The reading of this address was listened to by all the delegates and all the members of the Douma, and of the clerical synod. The division by Estates took place immediately after, and each order deliberated separately on the questions which the Government had proposed. The result of the discussions was presented to the Czar in writing separately by each Estate. The documents were drawn up by secretaries, specially attached for this purpose to the Assemblies of the different Estates. On two occasions only, in 1649 and 1682, were the members of the Sobor assembled in two different chambers, a higher and lower. The Upper House was formed by the Douma and the higher clergy, and the lower by the delegates of the lower orders. But the custom according to which each Estate deliberated separately, prevailed even on these two occasions, the higher and lower chambers being subdivided into as many sections as there were Estates.

In answering the demands of the Government, the delegates very often expressed their own sentiments as to the course of Russian politics. They complained bitterly of the wrongs done to the people by the officers of the State and judges; they pointed to the necessity of amending the whole executive and military administration; and by written petitions (*chelobitnia*), they insisted on the necessity of introducing certain amendments into the existing laws. The large part which these petitions played in the work of codifying the laws of Russia, a work which rendered illustrious the reign of Alexis Michaelovitch, has been amply recognised by recent inquirers, and especially by Ditiatin, Zagoskin, and Latkin.

The decisions to which the different Estates arrived were at the end of the session condensed into one single document, known under the name of *Zemskii prigovor*, which means the general verdict of the land. Several documents of this kind have been preserved. They are sealed, as a rule, with the seals of the Czar, of the Patriarch, and of the higher orders. As to the lower orders, their members kissed the cross in sign of approval.

Having thus considered the political history and internal constitution of the Sobors we will now examine the functions which they discharged. Foreign residents, and among them the well-known Fletcher, have noticed certain weak points in their organisation which prevented our representative Assemblies from rising to the level of English Parliaments. Fletcher makes the ingenious observation that the members of the Sobor had no right to present bills. This does not imply that the initiative of all reforms could proceed only from the Government; more than once the Estates complained of wrongs which were not mentioned in the address from the crown and asked for reforms which had not been thought of by the Government. But their right to petition the crown did not go further than that of the French Estates-General. Like them the Sobors were unable to provide for the fulfilment of their demands, and for the same reason which prevented the Estates-General of France from getting into their own hands the legal power. The right of initiating reforms, which the English Parliament began to exercise under the Lancastrian kings remained totally unknown in France as well as in Russia. At the time when the English Parliament were replacing petitions by bills, the French Estates continued to present their *cahiers de doléances*, leaving to the Government the right of taking in its *ordonnances* no notice whatever of their demands. The same was also the case in Russia, where new laws were directly decreed by the Czar and his Douma and the "general verdict of the land" remained for years and years inoperative.

If the Sobors only played a secondary part in matters of legislation, the control that they exercised over the executive machinery of the State was even less efficacious. I cannot mention a single case, in which royal councillors were removed and new persons appointed in their stead at the express desire of the Sobor. The Moscovite Government was, it is true, in no way a Parliamentary Government. Nevertheless the fact does not prove that the Sobors had nothing in common with English Parliaments or French States-General. We must not forget that mediæval Europe was, as a rule, ignorant of Parliamentary Government, and that Assemblies, like the Mad Parliament of Oxford or the revolutionary French Estates of 1355, both of which tried to establish a kind of cabinet, were but exceptions. Although the Sobor had no right to impose on the Czar the obligation of calling certain persons to his counsels, the part it took in the general politics of the country was a large one. We have had occasion to show that questions of war and peace were settled by its advice. Both the surrender of Asov and the annexation of Little Russia took place in compliance with its desires. And though the Sobor was denied the right of choosing the Ministry, it had a much higher right, that of choosing the Czars. On this point it had no grounds to envy either the English Parliaments, or the States-General of France.

So long as the new dynasty of the Romanovs remained faithful to the engagements entered into by the Czar Michael, that is to say during the first part of the seventeenth century, the voting subsidies was as much the function of the Russian representative Assembly as it was of the representative Assemblies of England, France, Germany, or Spain. During the greater part of the reign of the first Romanov no subsidy was levied, no benevolence extorted without the consent of the Sobor. This scrupulous observance of its financial authority required its periodical convocation just as much as the meeting of the English representatives was needed many years before the introduction of triennial and septennial parliaments. Excepting during the period just mentioned, the Sobors were summoned at irregular periods and only when the needs of the Government required their help.

Like other representative Assemblies they were convened and dissolved by the sovereign, and had no right to assemble according to their own will.

If we would know what good they have done to Russia we must study the part they have played in the removal of public grievances and the reform of justice. We must remember that more than once they opposed the oligarchical Government of the boyars, the local despotism of provincial Governors or *voivodes*, and the bribery and exactions of the bureaucracy of Moscow. We must remember how often they were the champions of justice and equality in opposing the system of judicial immunities, the extravagant donations of crown lands, and the exemption from taxation of the nobility and clergy. We shall then have no difficulty in acknowledging that their influence was truly beneficial. On several occasions they had the honour of participating in large administrative and judicial reforms, such as the codification of the law and the abolition of the abnormal custom by which offices in the army were held, not by men of ability and talent, but by those of aristocratic birth. Foreign politics were more than once treated by the Sobors with discernment and practical good sense. Their patriotic and religious feelings did not keep them from recognising the danger of a new war and the necessity of relinquishing a conquest which had been easily made. On the other hand their natural dislike of new taxes did not prevent them from stretching out a helping hand to their orthodox brethren in their endeavours to emancipate themselves from the religious persecution of Catholic Poland. Though they opposed on one occasion the annexation of Asov, nevertheless on another occasion these representatives of the people of Great Russia openly manifested their desire for union with Little Russia, notwithstanding the possibility of a new war that would necessarily be followed by an increase in taxation. In the so-called period of troubles they stood forth as the champions of the national idea by the opposition which they made to every political combination which might have resulted in the submission of Russia to a foreign prince. In those unhappy days when so many provinces were occupied by Polish and Swedish soldiers, and the boyars were half gained over to the interests of Vladislas, the son of the Polish king, when Novgorod made a separate peace with the Swedes, and was on the point of recognising the doubtful rights of a Swedish pretender, the political unity of Russia found champions only in the ranks of the lower orders represented at the Sobor.

The history of these old Russian Parliaments presents certainly a less dramatic interest than the history of English Parliaments or French States-General. Cases of conflict between the different orders convened to the National Councils occur very seldom. We read of no vehement invectives, like those which the deputies of the nobility thundered forth against the third estate at the *états generaux* of 1613. We hear also of no compacts or associations between estates, like those, which more than once allowed the English barons and burgesses to achieve a manifest victory over the king. The language employed by Russian representatives in speaking to their sovereign is moderate, and sometimes even servile. They like to call themselves the "slaves of his Majesty," but, in so doing, they never forget their obligations towards their electors, to open the eyes of the Government to "all the wrongs, depredations, and oppressions, committed by its officers." They are subjects, conscious of their duty towards sovereign and country, ready to sacrifice their life and estates for the defence of its essential interest ; they are not slaves, afraid of opening their mouths or of offending the ear of the monarch by a truthful description of their wrongs. Their loyalty towards the Czar finds a parallel in that which they entertain towards the Greek Church. They are orthodox, and, therefore, ready to shed their blood in the defence of their creed, simply represented, as it sometimes is, by the images of the saints ; but they have no inclination towards clericalism, and no objection to imposing taxes on the clergy and even to secularising their estates for the good of the country and the advantage of the military class. Illiterate as were their members, it is not surprising that the Sobors took no measure to increase the number of schools and educational establishments. They are probably the sole representative assemblies which never uttered a word about science or scholarship. It was chiefly due to their ignorance that their opinions about commercial intercourse with foreign countries were so little rational. It is not surprising if the whole policy of trade reduced itself, according to their understanding, to the elimination of the competition of the Eastern and Western merchants.

With such helpers as these no general reform, like that of Peter the Great, was likely to be accomplished. It may be easily understood, therefore, why this greatest of Russian revolutionists never tried to associate the Sobors in his work. The reforms at which he aimed: the subversion of the civil and military organisation, the introduction of a totally new provincial administration, copied from Swedish originals; of a standing army, like those of the French and German autocrats; the opening of Russian markets to the competition of foreign merchants; the establishment of technical schools and such like innovations, were not to be carried out by "the decision of the whole land," to employ the consecrated term for Russian legal enactments during the period directly preceding that of Peter the Great. "Enlightened despostism" found in Russia the same difficulty in going hand in hand with the old Assemblies of estates, as it did in Austria at the time of Joseph the Second.

Fully to understand the reasons which prevented the further development of the Russian national councils, we must also bear in mind that the period in which Russia, by the genius of Peter, was thrown into active intercouse with European powers, was far from being the golden age of representative Government. When the Sobors began to take root in the Russian soil, Parliaments and States-General were rapidly advancing to a state of complete annihilation or temporary suppression. What importance can we attach to the deliberations of the English Parliaments under the Tudors, or even under the Stuarts, up to the year 1640? What National Assembly can we mention in France after the year 1613? The fall of representative institutions, which we notice both in England and in France, was a common fact of European history. The German Reichstag and the Landstände of the different States which composed the Holy Roman Empire had fallen into the same state of political insignificance during the period following the treaty of Munster. The same fate had overtaken the Cortes of Castille and Aragon, and the provincial estates of Hungary and Bohemia. All over Europe monarchical power was steadily increasing, and autocracy becoming the ruling principle of the day. Was it likely, therefore, that Peter, who declared that he would willingly have given to Richelieu a good moiety of his dominions on condition of being taught by him how to rule the remainder, was it likely, I ask, that that same Peter should bring home from his long voyages in the West any particular respect for representative institutions? It is, therefore, easily understood why, from the beginning of the eighteenth century, the Sobors, without being abolished, should have ceased to be convened.

It was not until there was a general revival of representative institutions throughout Europe that Russian statesmen were found once more occupied with the question of the Sobors.

Alexander I., to judge by the liberality with which he endowed the Poles with a representative assembly, was, at least in the first part of his reign, not directly opposed to the idea of re-calling to life those venerable institutions of the past. Among the papers of his most intimate Councillor, Speransky, there has been found the project of a constitution, according to which the Council of State, this natural heir of the old Russian Douma, was to be strengthened by the introduction of representatives and notables, chosen from the different Estates of the Empire. In much more recent days a similar project was presented by Loris Melikoff to Alexander II., and an imperial ukase summoning this new Assembly of notables was already signed, when the premature death of the Emperor put an end to the expectations of the Liberal party. In the first weeks of his reign Alexander III. himself was not opposed to the idea of reviving the old national institution of the Sobors, and his first two ministers for Home Affairs, Loris Melikoff and Ignatiev, were both in favour of such a reform. It was only from the day when Count Dimitri Tolstoi took upon his shoulders the burthen of the home politics of Russia, that all thoughts were given up of convoking a representative assembly. The Government then entered on the fatal task of the subversion of all recent reforms. Nobody can tell how long will be the duration of the period of reaction upon which we have entered; but on the other hand nobody can doubt that the convocation of a national council is the most natural way of satisfying the wishes of the constantly increasing party of malcontents—a body of men which has been nick-named by its opponents "the Intelligent Party" (*intelligentia*)—a nick-name, which certainly cannot offend those on whom it is conferred.

The convocation of a national representative assembly would no doubt close the era of misunderstanding between the Russian people and the imperial power of the Czars; it would unite the Russian past with the present and future; and would once more open a large field to the co-operation of society for the redress of old wrongs and the establishment of personal liberty and social justice.

# LECTURE VI.

## THE ORIGIN, GROWTH, AND ABOLITION OF PERSONAL SERVITUDE IN RUSSIA.

An account of the origin, growth, and abolition of serfdom in Russia might easily be made to fill volumes, so vast and so various are the materials on which the study of it is based. But for the purpose now in view, that of bringing before your notice the general conclusion to which Russian historians and legists have come as to the social development of their country, perhaps a single lecture will suffice. In it I cannot pretend to do more than present to you those aspects of the subject on which the minds of Russian scholars have been specially fixed of late years.

Among the first to be considered is the origin of that system of personal servitude and bondage to the land in which the Russian peasant lived for centuries. An opinion long prevailed that this system was due solely to the action of the State, which, at the end of the sixteenth century, abolished the freedom of migration previously enjoyed by the Russian peasant and bound him for ever to the soil. This opinion, which would have made Russian serfdom an institution quite apart from that of the serfdom of the Western States of Europe, has been happily abandoned, and consequently its development becomes the more interesting, in so far as it discloses the action of those economic and social forces which produced the personal and real servitude of the so-called villein all over Europe.

Whilst stating the most important facts in the history of Russian serfdom, I shall constantly keep in view their analogy with those presented by the history of English or French villenage. By so doing I hope to render the natural evolution of Russian serfdom the more easily understood.

The first point to which I desire to call your attention is the social freedom enjoyed by the Russian peasant in the earlier portion of mediæval history. The peasant, then known by the name of *smerd* —from the verb *smerdet,* to have a bad smell—was as free to dispose of his person and property, as was the Anglo-Saxon *ceorl,* or the old German *mark-genosse.* He had the right to appear as a witness in Courts of Justice, both in civil and in criminal actions; he enjoyed the right of inheriting—a right, however, which was somewhat limited by the prevalence of family communism—and no one could prevent him from engaging his services to any landlord for as many years as he liked, and on terms settled by contract. Lack of means to buy a plough and the cattle which he needed for tilling the ground very often led the free peasant to get them from his landlord on condition that every year he ploughed and harrowed the fields of his creditor. It is in this way that an economic dependence was first established between two persons equally free, equally in possession of the soil, but disposing the one of a larger, the other of a smaller capital. The name under which the voluntary serf is known to the Pravda, the first legal code of Russia, is that of *rolcini zakoup;* this term signifies a person who has borrowed money on condition of performing the work of ploughing (*ralo* means the plough) so long as his debt remains unpaid.

The frequent want of the simplest agricultural implements, which Magna Charta designates as *contenementum*, was also probably the chief cause, which induced more than one Russian peasant to prefer the condition of a sort of French *métayer* or petty farmer, whose rent, paid in kind, amounts to a fixed proportion of the yearly produce, to that of a free shareholder in the open fields and village common. The almost universal existence of *métayage*, or farming on the system of half-profits, is now generally recognised. Thorold Rogers has proved its existence in mediæval England, and in France and Italy this system is still found. In saying this, I have particularly in view the French *champart* and the *mezzeria* of Tuscany.

The prevalence in ancient Russia of the same rude

and elementary mode of farming is established by numerous charters and contracts, some of which are as late as the end of the seventeenth century, whilst others go back to the beginning of the sixteenth. It would appear that previous to that date such contracts were not put into writing, apparently on account of the small diffusion of knowledge. We are therefore reduced to the necessity of presuming the existence of these contracts solely because the intrinsic causes which brought them into existence in the sixteenth century had been in operation for hundreds of years before. The peasant, on entering into such a contract, took upon himself the obligation of paying back in the course of time the money which had been lent to him—the "*serebro,*" silver, according to the expression used in contemporary documents. From the name of the capital intrusted to them (the *serebro*) arose the surname of *serebrenik,* which may be translated *silver-men,* under which peasants settled on a manor were generally known; their other being *polovnik,* or men paying half of their yearly produce to the lord, although as a rule their payments did not amount to more than a quarter. So long as his debt remained unpaid the *métayer* was obliged to remunerate the landlord by villein service performed on the demesne lands of the manor. According to the German writer Herberstein, who visited Russia in the seventeenth century, the agricultural labour which the *serebrenik* performed for the lord very often amounted each week to a six-days' service, at any rate in summer. Contracts still preserved also speak of other obligations of the *serebrenik*, very like those of the mediæval English socman. Such, for instance, were the obligations of cutting wood and of forwarding it on their own carts to the manor-house, and of paying certain dues on the occasion of the marriage of the peasant's daughter. I need not insist on the similarity which this last custom presents to the mediæval English and French *maritagium*, or *formariage*, so evident is the likeness between them. Custom also required the peasant to make certain presents to his lord at Christmas and Easter, or at some other yearly festival, such for instance as that of the Assumption of the Blessed Virgin.

The peasant who chose to settle on the land of a manorial lord got the grant of a homestead in addition to that of land, and this was the origin of a sort of house-rent called the *projivnoe*, which as a rule amounted yearly to the fourth part of the value of the homestead.

As to the land ceded by the landlord to the settler who wished to live on his manor, its use became the origin of another special payment, the *obrok*, which represented a definite amount of agricultural produce. The *obrok* was often replaced by the obligation of doing certain fixed agricultural labour on the demesne land of the manor.

As soon as the peasant had repaid the money borrowed from the manorial lord, and had discharged all the payments required from him for the use of his land and homestead, he was authorised by custom to remove wherever he liked, of course giving up to the squire his house and his share in the open fields of the manor. At first this right of removal could be exercised at any period of the year, but this being found prejudicial to the agricultural interests of the country certain fixed periods were soon established, at which alone such a removal was allowed. Usually the end of harvest was fixed as the time when new arrangements could be entered into with regard to future agricultural labour without causing any loss to the interests of the landlord. Not only in autumn, however, but also in spring, soon after Easter, manorial lords were in the habit of permitting the establishment of new settlers on their estates, and the withdrawal of those peasants who expressed a desire to leave.

The first *Soudebnik*, the legal code published by Ivan III. in 1497, speaks of the festival of Saint George, which according to the Russian calendar falls on the 26th of November, as a period at which all removals ought to take place. Those peasants who had not been fortunate enough to free themselves from all obligations to the manor by this period were obliged to remain another year on its lands; he who was unable to repay the lord the sum borrowed was reduced to the same condition as that of the insolvent farmers of the Roman *ager publicus*, who, according to Fustel de Coulanges, saw their arrears of debt changed into a perpetual rent called the *canon*, and their liberty of migration superseded by a state of continual bondage to the land they cultivated. No Russian historian has shown the analogy existing between the origin of the Roman colonatus and that of Russian serfdom so clearly as Mr. Kluchevsky, the eminent professor of Russian history in the University of Moscow. It is to him that we are indebted for the discovery of the fact that centuries before the legal and general abolition of the right of free migration a considerable number of peasants had thus ceased to enjoy that liberty. Such was the case of those so-called "silver-men from the oldest times," viz., *starinnii serebrenniki*, who during the sixteenth century were already deprived of the right of free removal from no other cause but the want of money, so that the only condition on which they could withdraw from the manor on which they were was that of finding some other landlord willing to pay the money they owed, and thereby acquiring the right to remove them to his own manor.

So long as the Russian power was geographically limited to the possession of the central provinces in the immediate neighbourhood of Moscow, and so long as the shores of the Volga and Dnieper suffered from almost periodical invasions of the Tartars, the Russian peasant who might wish to leave a manor could not easily have procured the land he required; but when the conquests of Ivan III. and Ivan the Terrible had reduced to naught the power of the

Tartars, and had extended the Russian possessions both to the East and to the South, the peasants were seized with a spirit of migration, and legislation was required to put a stop to the economic insecurity created by their continual withdrawal from the manors of Inner Russia to the Southern and Eastern steppes. It is, therefore, easy to understand why laws to prevent the possibility of a return of peasant migration were first passed, at least on a general scale, at this period. It is no doubt true that, even at the end of the fifteenth century, to certain monasteries were granted, among other privileges, that of being free from the liability of having their peasants removed to the estates of other landlords. A charter of the year 1478 recognises such a privilege as belonging to the monks of the monastery of Troitzko-Sergievsk, which is, according to popular belief, one of the most sacred places in Russia. The financial interests of the State also contributed greatly to the change. The fact that the taxpayer was tied to the soil rendered the collection of taxes both speedier and more exact. These two causes sufficiently explain why, by the end of the sixteenth century, the removal of peasants from manor to manor had become very rare.

The system of land endowments in favour of the higher clergy and monasteries, and also of persons belonging to the knightly class, had increased to such an extent that, according to modern calculation, two-thirds of the cultivated area was already the property either of ecclesiastics or of secular grandees. It is therefore easy to understand why, during the sixteenth century, the migratory state of the Russian agricultural population came to be considered as a real danger to the State by the higher classes of Russian society. The most powerful of the nobles and gentry did their best to retain the peasants on their lands. Some went even farther, and, by alleviating the burdens of villein-service, and securing a more efficient protection for them from administrative oppression, induced the peasants who inhabited the lands of smaller squires to leave their old homes and settle on their manors. It was in order to protect the small landowners from this sort of oppression that Boris Goudonov, the all-powerful ruler of Russia in the reign of Theodor Ivanovitch, promulgated a law, according to which every one was authorised to insist on the return of a peasant who left his abode, and that during the five years next following his departure. This law was promulgated in 1597. As no mention is made in it of the right previously enjoyed by the peasants of removing from one manor to another on St. George's Day, this law of 1597 has been considered by historians as the direct cause of the introduction of the so-called "bondage to the soil" (*krepostnoie pravo*). Such was certainly not its object. The right of migration on the Day of St. George was openly acknowledged by the laws of 1601 and 1602. The bondage of the peasant to the soil became an established fact only in the year 1648, when the new code of law, the so-called *Oulogienie* (chap. xi.), refused to any one the right to receive on his lands the peasant who should run away from a manor, and abolished that limit of time beyond which the landlord lost the right to reclaim the peasant who had removed from his ancient dwelling.

The number of serfs rapidly increased during the second half of the seventeenth and the eighteenth centuries, owing to the prodigality with which the Czars and Emperors endowed the members of the official class with lands, in disregard often of their previous occupation by free village communities, the members of which were forced to become the serfs of the persons who received the grant. It is in this way that Catherine II., for instance, during the thirty-four years of her reign, increased the number of serfs by 800,000 new ones, and that Paul I., in a period of four years, added 600,000 to the number, which was already enormous.

Before the reign of Catherine, serfdom was almost unknown in Little Russia, where it had been abolished by Bogdan Chmelnitzky, soon after the separation of Little Russia from Poland, and in the Ukraine (the modern Government of Kharkov), where it had never before existed. In 1788 she revoked the right hitherto enjoyed by the peasants of these two provinces to remove from one manor to another. The same right of free removal was abolished a few years later in the "Land of the Don Kossacks" and among the peasants of the Southern Governments, called New Russia (*Novorossia*).

But if the second part of the eighteenth century saw the territorial extension of serfdom over almost all the Empire, it was also the period in which first began the movement which led to emancipation. From France came the first appeals for the liberation of the serfs. In 1766 the Society of Political Economists founded in Petersburg on the model of the agricultural societies of France was asked by the Empress to answer the question: "Whether the State would be benefited by the serf becoming the free owner of his land?" Marmontel and Voltaire considered it to be their duty to express opinions in favour of a partial abolition of serfdom. Marmontel thought that the time was come to supersede villein-service by a sort of hereditary copyhold. Voltaire went a step farther, inviting the Empress to liberate immediately the serfs on the Church lands. As to the rest, free contract alone ought to settle the question of their emancipation. Another Frenchman much less known, the legist Beardé de l'Abaye, gave it as his opinion that the Government should maintain a strict neutrality towards the question of serfdom. It ought to be abolished only by free contract between landlords and serfs, the former endowing the latter with small parcels of land. In this way the serf would become a private owner, so that in case he should rent any land from the squire, the squire would be able to seize the peasant's plot in case of non-payment of his rent. Diderot was the only Frenchman who acknowledged the necessity of an immediate abolition of personal servitude; but in his letters to the Empress he does not say a single word about the necessity for securing to the liberated serf at least a small portion of the manorial land.

Although Catherine II. was willing to be advised by the Encyclopedists as to the way in which serfdom might be abolished, she took effectual means to prevent the expression of Russian public opinion on the same subject. A memorial presented to the Petersburg Society of Political Economists by a young Russian author called Polenov was not allowed to appear in print, for no other reason than that it contained a criticism on the existing system of serfdom.* The author of the memorial did not demand the immediate abolition of this old wrong; he only wanted to see it replaced by a sort of perpetual copyhold. The Government was more severe towards another Russian writer, Radischev, who was the first to advocate not only the personal liberty of the serf, but also his endowment with land. The work of Radischev † appeared in 1789, several years after the suppression of the insurrectionary movement of Pougachev, but it was regarded as a sort of commentary on the demand for "liberty and land,"

* Compare V. Semevsky, "The Peasant Question in Russia during the Eighteenth and Nineteenth Century," Petersburg, 1888.

† "The Voyage from Petersburg to Novgorod."

which the Russian peasant had addressed to that leader, who had answered it by a solemn promise that he would make the serf free and prosperous. Catherine not only ordered the immediate suppression of the work of Radischev, but brought the author before the Courts of Justice, accusing him of being a traitor to his country. Radiscnev was condemned to death; but this penalty was commuted to perpetual banishment to Siberia.

It was not till the reign of Alexander the First that the Russian Government began to take effectual measures to ameliorate the social condition of the serf. According to the account given by those immediately around him, and especially by Adam Czartorysky, Alexander was an avowed friend of peasant emancipation. He gave his firm support to the proposed law giving the landlords the right to liberate their serfs, and even to endow them with shares in the open fields if they paid for them. In 1803 this law was passed, and 47,000 serfs were soon after enfranchised, and became a separate class under the name of the "free agriculturists." Sixteen years later (in 1819) the enfranchisement of the serf became an accomplished fact in the three Baltic provinces, the peasant obtaining the free disposal of his person on condition of abandoning to his landlord the parcels of ground previously in his possession. This reform was accomplished in the same manner as that carried out in 1812 by Napoleon in the Kingdom of Poland. In the thoroughly Russian provinces no direct measures were at this time taken to abolish the legal servitude of the peasant, but the question was more than once debated in private circles and by learned bodies. In the year 1812, for instance, the Petersburg Society of Political Economists declared that it would give 2000 roubles to the author of the best treatise on the question of the relative advantages of free and servile labour in agriculture. This question by itself shows the influence which Adam Smith's "Wealth of Nations," which had been translated into Russian in 1803, was beginning to exercise on Russian thought. Nine treatises were forwarded to the Society, of which three only were in favour of the further maintenance of servile labour. But the greater number expressed the opinion that the enfranchisement of the serf, provided that he was allowed to keep the land he occupied, would be of great advantage to the landlord himself. This idea, in conformity to which serfdom had been abolished in the Baltic provinces, was the expression of a fact quite familiar to the student of economic history. The work of an enslaved labourer is never so productive as that of a free labourer. So long as rent is low, as certainly was the case in Russia in past centuries, the work of the serf is by no means fairly recompensed by the land he owns. But in the first quarter of the nineteenth century, when Russia began to be considered as the granary of Europe, on account of the vast exports of wheat from her ports, rent rapidly rose, and this rise produced a complete change in the relative value of servile work and the land which was in the possession of the peasant.

The question put by the Society of Political Economists could not, therefore, possibly have received any other answer than that given to it by the majority of the authors who sent in papers to the Society. Serfdom was rapidly becoming a burden on the manorial lords themselves, as many of them began to be conscious. The barons of the Baltic shore were the first to understand the advantage which the liberation of the serf, followed by a resumption of the ground he owned, would have on their class interests. The nobility of Toula and Riasan, as well as that of Dinabourg, Petersburg, and Czarskoie Selo, seemed also to become conscious of this fact, for they petitioned the Emperor Nicholas to establish local committees who might prepare the outlines of a new emancipation act. Among the nobles immediately surrounding the Czar, Prince Mentchikov expressed his opinion of the desirability and advantage of freeing the peasant and at the same time of enriching the landlord by leaving in his hands all those shares in the common ground which had been held by the peasants. The interests of the nobility certainly required the establishment of a class similar to that of the English labourers, but the peasants were naturally averse to any change which would lessen their hold on the soil. In 1812 a peasant rising took place in the Government of Pensa, the revolted serfs expressing their wants by the old motto "Liberty and Land." In 1826 again the same motto was the watchword of another rising, this time provoked by a rumour that land and liberty would shortly be secured to the serfs.

Under the influence of this clear expression of the people's wants, the Government of Nicholas abandoned all idea of emancipation which was not to be followed by the endowment of the peasant with land. Not daring, as he openly acknowledged, to lay hands on the sacred rights of private property by liberating the serfs and making them free owners of the soil, Nicholas proposed to alter the existing condition of the serf by making him a sort of copyholder or perpetual tenant of small parcels of manorial ground, on condition of the payment of perpetual rent. In the Polish provinces, such copyhold tenures, very like the French *censives*, were already in existence. The Government, therefore, only extended a system which already existed when, in 1842, they ordered the preparation in each manor of a sort of registry, called "inventory," in which the amount of payments in kind and money, made by the serfs to the landlord, were to be inscribed, in order that in future no other levies might be made.

Neither of these two schemes for amending the untenable position of the serf was good enough to obtain the approbation of those to whom, at this time, actually belonged the guidance of public opinion. It will be to the eternal honour of the Russian press that it constantly preached in favour of a reform which would at once liberate the serf and make him legal owner of the shares of manorial ground which were already in his possession. Among the persons directly implicated in the insurrectionary movement of the 24th of December 1825, two, Pestel and Jakoushkine, had already declared themselves to be supporters of such a scheme.

The diffusion of socialist ideas greatly contributed to strengthen among the literary class the persuasion that it would be impossible to liberate the serf otherwise than by endowing him with land. The well-known plot which was organised by Petroschevsky, among its other aims, had that of allotting parcels of ground to the liberated serf. The great exile Herzen, in a Russian newspaper then published in London, openly expressed his opinion that the common ownership of the land should be retained in the hands of the enfranchised peasant; and among the many schemes of emancipation, which circulated in the form of manuscript during the latter part of Nicholas's reign, more than one advocated the necessity of retaining the ancient ties which bound the peasant to the soil by making him the legal owner of his share in the open fields.

The "providential mission" of the Czar Alexander the Second was therefore disclosed in a state of society which was already prepared to accept the general outlines of a social reform, the end of which would be not only to liberate, but also to enrich, the peasant. As soon as Alexander ascended the throne rumours began to be circulated as to the approaching abolition of serfdom. The unexpected death of his father placed him on the throne at a moment of great and general depression, occasioned by the defeat of the Russian military forces under the walls of Sebastopol. The young Emperor made an eloquent appeal to the patriotism of his subjects, inviting them to increase the means of defence by a voluntary levy of a kind of militia, known under the name of *Opolcheme.* This measure strengthened the belief in the nearness of social and political reforms. The peasants, enrolled in the self-raised regiments of the militia, began to think that their more or less voluntary sacrifice of life and fortune would be rewarded by a complete liberation from the ignominious bonds of personal servitude. Crowds of serfs asked to be admitted into the militia, expecting to attain freedom in this way.

When the Peace of Paris was signed, and the peasants of the militia were ordered to return to their daily tasks, they openly expressed their belief that the charters by which the Emperor had liberated them from bondage were concealed by their landlords. These rumours produced great excitement. The years 1854 and 1855 are notorious for a series of local rebellions. These insurrections took place partly on the shores of the Volga, which had already felt, in the time of Catherine the Second, the horrors of a *jacquerie,* partly in some Central and South-western Governments, such as Vladimir,

Riasan, Tambov, Pensa, Voronej, and Kiev. These revolutionary movements, directed exclusively against the feudal aristocracy, produced a great impression on the Czar Alexander. Addressing the chiefs of the Moscovite nobility (the so-called marshals), the Czar showed his appreciation of the wants of the time by the following words: "Gentlemen, you surely understand yourselves the impossibility of retaining, without alteration and change, the existing mode of owning souls [a usual expression, the meaning of which is the right to the unpaid work of the serfs]. It is better to abolish personal servitude by legislative measures than to see it abolished by a movement from below. I ask you to consider such measures as might forward this end." These promising words, although followed by a direct declaration that serfdom was not to be abolished at once, strengthened the expectations of those who thought that the new reign would inaugurate an era of wide social and political reform. Although the Governor-General of Moscow, Zakrevsky, did his best to persuade the nobility that all projects concerning the abolition of serfdom were laid aside, it very soon appeared that such was by no means the intention of the Czar; for during the coronation the Home Secretary, Lanskoy, by the direct command of Alexander, entered into communication with those noblemen who were present in Moscow, in order to ascertain what were their opinions as to the best means of bringing about an amelioration in the actual condition of the serfs. These negotiations left no doubt as to the animosity with which the nobility of Great Russia considered every plan tending to the emancipation of the peasant. This induced the Minister to turn his eyes to those provinces in which the idea of liberating the serfs had taken root at the time when personal servitude had been abolished by Napoleon I. in the neighbouring districts of Poland, particularly the Governments of Vilna, Kovno, and Grodno. The Lithuanian nobles were already favourable to the idea, and were easily induced by the Governor-General Nasimov to present to the Czar an address asking for the abolition of bondage, but at the same time demanding exclusive possession of the land for the nobility. You therefore see that the conditions on which the Lithuanian nobles wanted to see the enfranchisement carried out were the same as those on which it had been already carried out in Poland and the Baltic provinces. Seeing the difficulty of preserving for their own profit the unpaid services of the peasant, they were anxious to secure to themselves the monopoly of the soil. The serf was to be allowed to become a free person only on condition of remaining a proletarian, living exclusively on the wages he earned. Carried out on such conditions, the emancipation would hardly have met with the approval of those who were most directly concerned. As far back as the reign of the Empress Catherine the peasant had plainly declared that he wanted not only liberty, but land. He was mindful of his ancient state, previous to that of bondage, which, as we have already shown, was the state of an owner in common of the ground he made fruitful by his work. No power on earth would have been strong enough to break the ties, centuries old, which united him to the soil. It was no doubt in the interests of the nobility to see these ties broken, for who could be the gainers in a scheme which promised enhancement of the mercantile value of the soil and cheap labour, if not those who had secured to themselves the monopoly of the property in land? What, on the other hand, was the liberated proletarian to become if not a labourer, given up to eternal toil on the estates of a land-monopolising nobility, and bound to receive from their hands those bare wages which would cover the expense of his existence? The Emperor and some persons in his confidence, were conscious of the social evils which the execution of such a plan would produce. It will be to the eternal glory of Alexander to have answered the request of the Lithuanian nobility by a decree by which, whilst allowing the establishment of local committees for the elaboration of measures which might achieve the emancipation in view, he plainly declared that the liberated serfs ought to be secured at least in the possession of their homesteads and of the land belonging to these homesteads (the so-called homestead-land — *ousadebnaiia zemlia*). This expression was obscure and ambiguous, for it was not easy to establish the limits of the so-called homestead-land. Was it to be considered as a compound of all the various communal privileges of which the peasant was possessed, or to mean only the ground directly surrounding his habitation? This question remained unsettled.

In the winter of 1851 the nobility of Petersburg, not wishing to remain behind that of Lithuania, presented to the Emperor an address very like the one just mentioned. This address and the decree it provoked deserve to be mentioned, for they show, on one hand, the desire of the aristocracy to preserve not only all the advantages of a land-owning class, but also to a certain extent the social dependence under which the peasant had lived towards them during the preceding centuries; and, on the other hand, the firm decision of the Government to secure to the peasant at least his property in the homestead he occupied, and in the land which surrounded it. The decree is curious too as a precise statement of the conditions on which the Government intended at first to accomplish the difficult task of emancipation. They are, as you will soon perceive, very different from those on which the emancipation was actually performed. No question is made of the direct interference of the State in order to buy back from the nobleman the plots of ground occupied by the serfs. This end is to be alone attained by way of free agreement between the parties. As long as this agreement has not taken place the serf is to continue to perform the agricultural labour and make the money payments fixed by law. The nobleman, on the other hand, exercises, as in the past, a kind of feudal justice and police. The ground of the whole manor is declared to be his property; the peasant is to receive no other endowment but that of his homestead.

The nobility of Nijni-Novgorod, that of Moscow, and of several other provinces, soon after this presented demands not very unlike those already mentioned. They were answered in the same way, and local committees, composed of noblemen, were accordingly formed, in order to elaborate the outlines of the intended reform in accordance with the views of the Government as already stated. These outlines were to be sent for further examination to a central board, which was first appointed on January 8, 1858, and was known under the name of the "Principal Committee on the Peasant Question." They were also to be the subject of careful study on the part of a newly opened section of the Board of Statistics. Men of radical ideas, such as Nicolas Miliutine and Soloviev, were included among its members. The reactionary party, on the other hand, counted more than one member in the "Principal Committee on the Peasant Question," a fact which induced the Government to detach from this Committee two especial sections, the so-called "Committee for the Drawing-up of the Reform Project," and that of "The Elaboration of Financial Measures, needed to secure the Execution of the Plan in View." The guidance of both Committees and the election of their members were entrusted to General Rostovzov, an avowed friend of the intended reform. An important change was introduced into the working of the bureaucratic machinery by the fact that some elected members of the provincial committees were allowed to have a seat at the meetings of the central bodies, and to exercise there the functions of experts. Among the persons so appointed we find several well-known Slavophiles, such as Samarin and Tcherkasky.

The work the central committees had to perform was, first of all, the drawing-up of a concise statement of the results attained by the deliberations of the local committees; next, the discussion of the different opinions which these latter had expressed; and, finally, the drawing-up of the conclusions to which the members of the central committees themselves had arrived. The members of the committees enjoyed the hitherto unknown freedom of expressing their opinion, and of consulting all sorts of papers and books, not excluding even those published by Russian emigrants. One of the members protesting against the idea of drawing information from the *Kolokol*, a Russian newspaper published in London by the political refugee Herzen, the President said that, according to his opinion, truth was to be taken into account, whoever might have expressed it. The formalism and official subordination so much observed by our bureaucracy were for the first time laid aside, and each member frankly expressed his views, however much they might be opposed to those of the President. The committee even went so far as to accept on certain points decisions which were not in accordance with the Imperial decrees. The local committee appointed by the nobility of Tver was the first to express the opinion that the peasants ought to be endowed with land beyond that which surrounded their homesteads. This opinion was endorsed by the central committee, which maintained that, although it was contradictory to the letter of the Imperial decrees, it was in perfect correspondence with their spirit.

On another occasion the "Committee for the Drawing-up of the Scheme of Reform" showed the same independence by adopting the view first put forward by members of the press, that it was necessary that the Government should come forward to buy up the land which the nobleman was called upon to surrender to the peasants of his manor. Now this view was quite the reverse of that expressed by the Imperial decrees we have previously cited.

In the whole of the movement the large and important part played by the public press is most striking. No doubt can be entertained that at its beginning the officials to whom was entrusted the elaboration of the plan were profoundly ignorant of the bearings of the question. The President of the Committee, General Rostovzov, frankly acknowledged this ignorance, and in his private correspondence with the Czar betrayed his fears of a national bankruptcy as the certain result of the Government taking on itself the redemption of the lands which were to be ceded to the peasants—fears which seem almost ludicrous now that this redemption has been effected, and the financial interests of the State have not suffered even for a moment.

A well-known Russian economist, Professor Ivanukoff,* has tried to show to what extent the press shared with the Government the difficult task of elaborating the scheme, according to which the serfs were to obtain "freedom and land." He is quite correct when he says that, with the exception of a single paper called the *Journal of Landed Proprietors*, the whole Russian Press unanimously declared itself in favour, not only of the abolition of personal servitude, but also of the endowment of the peasants with land. Such writers as Katkof, the well-known editor of the *Moscow Gazette*, a man who has lately played so prominent a part in the reactionary movement, were then the open friends of Liberalism, and rivalled the most advanced reformers in their defence of civil freedom. The opinions of Katkof were so greatly at variance with those of the Government at the beginning of the movement, that he was obliged to bring to a close a series of articles on the social condition of the serfs which he had begun in

* See his work, entitled "The Fall of Bondage in Russia," Petersburg, 1883.

his periodical, the *Russian Courier*. Another eminent publicist, Koschelev, who was the author of one of the numerous private schemes of emancipation (their number amounted to sixty-one), was obliged at the same time to abandon the further publication of a journal called the *Welfare of the Country*, on account of the strong language in which he advocated the endowment of the liberated serf with those portions of the land already in his possession. A Russian magazine of great renown, the *Contemporary*, was at the same time on the point of being suppressed on account of an article written by Professor Kavelin, expressing his views as to the opportuneness of redeeming the lands actually possessed by the peasants, and that, too, with the direct help of the State. The Minister of Public Instruction, Evgraf Kovalevsky, was even asked to issue a circular, by which the censorship was entrusted with the power of suppressing any article, pamphlet, or book, dealing with the question of enfranchisement, that had not previously been approved by the central committee. This untimely warfare against public opinion and the liberty of the press, fortunately enough, did not last long. The circular was printed in April, 1858, and seven months later the Government relaxed the restrictions imposed; and that because of the complete change in its own views as to the outlines of the reform. The opinions recently suppressed became those of the Government, and the prosecuted writers were considered, for a while at least, its surest allies.

I insist on these facts, because I know of no instance which better characterises the ordinary proceedings of the Russian bureaucracy. It begins, as a rule, by suppressing all that lies in its way, and then, finding no other issue, it adopts the line of conduct which it has recently condemned. A foreigner who has no notion of this mode of procedure must find great difficulty in understanding how it happens that in a country where no freedom of the press is recognised, in which generals and high officials seem alone to have the right of professing opinions on public matters, the press, nevertheless, has more than once exercised a decisive influence on the course of politics. The all-powerful bureaucracy is very often but an empty-headed fool, anxious to accept the ideas of the despised and prosecuted journalist. In Russia, as well as everywhere else, the true and lasting power is that of public opinion, and of those who know how to influence it. Periods in which the Government acts contrary to public opinion occur from time to time. They are very harmful to those who dare to remain faithful to their opinions. For a while nothing is heard of but the need of suppression both of opinions and of those who publicly profess them. But time passes and the Government begins to reap the fruits of its own sowing. At every step it takes, it finds on the part of those it governs nothing but ill-will, a hidden but profound mistrust. As soon as it feels that it is losing all hold on the minds and hearts of the people, it is the first to condemn what it has recently praised. Some fine morning everybody is startled by learning that the very men who had done their best to render impossible the public expression of certain ideas are now drawing their inspiration from these same ideas.

But I feel that I have made perhaps a necessary, but at all events a too long, digression from the direct line of my inquiries. I will therefore return to them at once, and begin by pointing out those points on which the committee appointed to elaborate the law of enfranchisement carried out in their scheme—the opinions of the press.

It was the press which first advocated the notion that the liberated peasant ought to become the owner of the land actually in his possession. Schemes for realising this idea had been already worked out in the reign of Nicholas by some patriotic scholars and publicists. Among them was Professor Kavelin, whose project was published by the Russian *Contemporary*, at the head of other articles, on the impending reform. It was on Kavelin that first fell the responsibility of expressing ideas in opposition to the views of the Government. His opinion as to the necessity of endowing the peasant with land soon found an echo in the debates of the nobility of Tver, who petitioned the Czar to extend his promise concerning grants of land to the enfranchised serf, not only to his homestead and the ground surrounding it, but also to the shares the peasant possessed in the open fields of the village. In giving an account of the different opinions expressed by the provincial nobility, the central committee referred to this scheme proposed by the nobility of Tver, and recommended it to the Government. Thus we see how prominent a part the press played on this occasion.

Its influence was no less powerful in the question on what principle should be based the future ownership exercised by the peasants. Two schemes, widely differing from each other, were at the same time proposed by the press. The one (chiefly supported by economists such as Vernadsky, and publicists like Katkof) recommended the immediate acceptance of measures favourable to the development of private property; the other (supported by the majority of the Slavophile and Radical press) was in favour of the strict maintenance of the village community system, with its periodical redistribution of land. On this question. Slavophiles such as Samarin and Koschelev went hand in hand with the Socialist Tchernishevsky, the author of the very remarkable essay on the "Prejudices of Political Economists against the Common Ownership in Land," an essay which forms the base of the social creed of the so-called Nihilists.

The project of emancipation elaborated by Government officials is a sort of compromise between these contradictory opinions. It starts with the idea of a temporary maintenance of the common ownership in land, but advocates certain measures favourable to the development of private property. A new re-distribution of the shares is allowed only when it is demanded by two-thirds of the persons voting at the village Assembly. Every person paying back to the Government the money advanced to him, in order to remunerate the landlord for the ground he has been obliged to yield, is immediately acknowledged to be the private proprietor of his share. The scheme of the Slavophiles and the Radicals required a simple majority to make legal the village decision concerning a new re-distribution of the land; they were, and are still, opposed to the recognition of private property on the part of the peasant who has bought back his share in the common land.

Very important, too, was the service rendered by the press on the important question of the amount of land which the feudal lord should be required to leave in the hands of his liberated serfs. Most writers were in favour of leaving to the peasants the quantity of land they actually occupied; "for," said they, and not without reason, "this amount must, no doubt, correspond to the necessities of their existence, as the amount has been accorded to them by the landlord for no other purpose but that of merely supporting life." Few advocated the desirability of establishing in each province a certain maximum and minimum of land dotation. The members of the central committee were favourable to the first scheme; and if the last prevailed, and found its expression in the law, the explanation is to be found in the opposition which the first plan met with on the part of the nobility and their chief supporters in the higher official circles.

One important question arose, whether the landlord should still keep a certain executive authority within the limits of the township; or whether the inner life of the village was thenceforth to be subject to no other rules than those issued by the village Assembly, and put in force by its elected chiefs, the elders or *starostas*. The press almost unanimously expressed its desire to see the realisation of the latter plan. The country people, said the press, required complete liberty, or, to use the popular expression, "pure liberty." Now, this liberty was inconsistent with the maintenance of rights such as those exercised by the German noblemen in the Baltic provinces or the *junkers* of Eastern Prussia. The only way to render any revival of personal servitude impossible was to establish the system of peasant self-government. Opinions differed on the question as to whether the landlord ought to be a member of the township or not. The Radicals were against it, and the Slavophiles did not attach great importance to it, thinking that the landlord would feel himself quite isolated amid the crowd of his former subjects. The Liberals alone were favourable to the idea of increasing the number of township members by admitting all residents, without distinction of class, to vote in the village Assembly. Their advice did not prevail, and the commune became a class institution, to the great disadvantage both of the peasants and of the whole State.

One of the most difficult points was undoubtedly that of fixing the amount of remuneration which the landlord ought to receive, not for the loss of his right over the person of his former serf, but for that of the land he was obliged to cede in his favour. The question was the more difficult because the land, in more than one part of Russia, had really no market price at all, the nobility and gentry being alone allowed to bid for it. The press, reasonably enough, insisted on the necessity of establishing a correspondence between the revenue the peasant got from his share and the amount of remuneration paid for it to the landlord. But such was not the opinion, either of the central or local committees; and we must lay on their shoulders the responsibility of the fact, that it was the amount of payments in kind and the quantity of villein-service performed by the peasant, which were selected as the base of valuation. This certainly was against the interests of the peasant, highly overcharged as he was by the manorial lord, who obliged him to pay rents much surpassing the revenue of the land he cultivated. By not adopting on this point the views entertained by the press, the reformers, as you easily see, did a great social injustice.

It was the press also which first agitated the question of the desirability of the direct interference of the Government, in order to facilitate the expropriation of the nobleman in favour of the peasants. The head of the central committee, Rostovzov, as we have already seen, thought the financial difficulties of such a measure insurmountable. Such was not the opinion of the press, which predicted that the issue of "rentes," or Government bonds, securing to the landlord a certain percentage on the capital which he should cede to the peasant in the form of land, would not lower the value of the paper money already in circulation. It was fortunate that in the end this method was adopted, for the prophecy was not only realised, but the interests of agriculture, and consequently of the country generally, were considerably advanced by the capital paid in the form of these bonds to the expropriated landlords. More than one great landowner was deeply in debt at the time emancipation took place; very few had the capital needed for the economic arrangements required for the substitution of the paid work of the free peasant for the unpaid work of the serf. They obtained it by selling or mortgaging the "rentes" or bonds paid to them by the Government.

We therefore find that on all points the press was the guide, the authoritative adviser, the sure ally of the Government. This last character plainly appeared in the struggle which the central committee had to maintain with the delegates of the provincial Committees. These bodies were composed exclusively of members of the local nobility, and were empowered to present their opinions on the impending reform. Unconscious of the alteration which had taken place in the intentions of the Government, they expressed ideas in complete accord with those at first entertained by the Emperor. The majority in each committee, seeing that it was impossible under present circumstances to maintain their old rights over the person of the serf, consented to recognise his freedom, and that without pay. They were anxious about one thing alone—to retain as far as possible in their own hands the land actually possessed by the peasant. This feeling was the stronger where the soil was rich, as was the case in the Central and Southern Governments, where the black soil prevails. It was less so in the west and north, where the ground yielded but a small rent. We find a complete unanimity between the utterances of the central and southern nobles, both insisting on the necessity of limiting the expropriation of the land in favour of the peasants to that occupied by their homesteads, whilst in the north more than one committee consented to extend this to the arable land and the undivided common.

The provincial committees were almost unanimous (I speak of course only of the majority of their members) in their request that the individual shares of each peasant household should be readjusted according to a certain maximum and minimum fixed for each province. Many a committee insisted on the maintenance of feudal police, if not of feudal justice, and all showed an equal interest in the suppression of the uncontrolled power of the bureaucracy in matters of provincial administration.

The minorities of almost every committee, who were more or less influenced by the press, approached much more nearly in their request to the views entertained by the majority in the central committee. They gave their consent to the plan of expropriating in favour of the peasants a part of the noblemen's lands; they insisted on the participation of the Government in the act of redeeming the area formerly allotted by the landlords to the serfs of their respective manors; they strongly opposed the scheme of a transitory state in which the peasant, unable to buy back the land he owned, was condemned to continue his villein service and his feudal dues or payments in kind. At the same time they put forward certain general demands which went much beyond the promises already given by the Government. They made requests for a general change in the existing system of provincial administration. According to these bureaucracy should give place to a system of local self-government. They insisted on the necessity of amending the deficient judicial organisation. They demanded trial by jury and liberty of the press. Some of the members went even so far as to draw up a resolution in favour of the general representation of the people and the revival of the ancient system of National Councils, the *Sobors*.

We must not lose sight of these political requirements if we wish to understand why it was that the Government, as soon as the deputies both of the majority and the minority of provincial committees were assembled in Petersburg, hindered their general meetings. It was but separately that each of the delegates was admitted to put forward his requests, and to give oral advice to the members of the general committee. This mistrust on the part of the Government embittered more than one of the delegates against the members of the central committee, and threw them into the arms of that minority which, in the central committee itself, defended the interests of the nobility. It was chiefly composed of the "Marshal" of the Petersburg nobility, Count Peter Schouvalov, Mr. Aprakasin, who occupied the same post in the Government of Orel, and Mr. Posen, the delegate of Pultawa. These three gentlemen insisted on the desirability of keeping the land in the hands of the nobility, and of granting to the peasantry only a sort of soccage-tenure, or "censive," on the land they occupied. Whilst the majority of the committee insisted on the direct interference of the Government in the redemption of the noblemen's land, and the propriety of putting an end to villein-service, at any rate after a period of twelve years, these gentlemen were in favour of leaving to a free contract, entered into by the manorial lord and his former serfs, the difficult task of settling their future relations. It was in the house of Schouvalov that the discontented delegates regularly assembled; it was there that they drew up this protest against the action of the central committee and the so-called "encroachments of the bureaucracy." Their appeal, made in the form of a pamphlet, published in Leipsig, and addressed to the new delegates summoned to Petersburg from the provinces not hitherto represented, found a ready hearing, and the Government encountered in these new helpers even a larger amount of mistrust and ill-will than that already shown by their predecessors.

This time the opposition of the nobility was of much greater consequence. General Rostovzov, whose influence over the Czar was very great, died suddenly, before the completion of the work entrusted to his care, and Count Panin, an avowed foe to the action of the committee, became its President. He did his best to induce the members to abandon their former decision; and it is only to the firmness of character shown by men like Nicholas Milutine, that we are indebted for the strict maintenance of the general outlines of the form already elaborated. Finding himself powerless to change the decisions of the committee, Panin tried to arouse some opposition to the scheme published by it, among the ranks of that general committee of which the committee for the elaboration of the law of emancipation was but a section. He tried to achieve the same ends in the Council of State, where the scheme of the new law had finally to be discussed. Happily the time allowed for the debates was very limited, as the Government insisted on the immediate realisation of the long-promised "liberty." They lasted in the general committee but a few months, while in the Council of State they were limited to a fortnight. It is due to this fact that neither of the two boards introduced very extensive amendments in the emancipation law. Those they did make were all in favour of the nobility. The most mischievous consisted in the considerable diminution of the maximum and minimum shares accorded to the peasant, and in the resolution that no rights would be recognised as belonging to the villagers in the common pastures of the manor. The interests of the peasants were also sacrificed in the permission which was given to the landlords to diminish the shares of the peasants, on the condition of renouncing all remuneration for the ground which they ceded. In all these measures the demands of the nobles were complied with.

But the great ends at which the reformers aimed, the liberation, that is to say, of the peasant from all personal dependence on the manorial lord, and the securing to him the right of possessing land in common, were nevertheless attained. The law of February 19, 1861, was the beginning of a new era —an era of democratic development, as well as of economic and social growth, for the immense Empire of the Czars. For there is no doubt about the vast influence which the law of 1861 has exercised in all directions. It is that which made more than twenty millions of people at once the free disposers of their own destinies and the communistic owners of the land. Villein services, rents in kind and in money, feudal monopolies, and manorial jurisdiction, ceased to exist, and the peasant became the member of a self-governing body, or the *Mir*. The ideas of social justice and of equality before the law—ideas hitherto cherished but by a few dreamers such as Radischev and Herzen, or revolutionists like those so-called "Decembrists," who organised the rebellion of December 24, 1825—made their triumphant entry into the Russian world, working a complete change in the organisation of public schools, admitting the son of the peasant to sit side by side with the son of the nobleman and the merchant in the same grammar school and the same university, revolutionising both official circles and the drawing-room, admitting to both persons of low birth but high education.

The emancipation of the serf certainly was not carried out without some loss to the landowning gentry, but the squire soon recovered from the state into which he was brought by his inexperience in the management of his estate without the help of unpaid servants. Capital was invested in land; agricultural machines were introduced; the yearly income began to rise rapidly, and with it the value of the land was augmented. It was partly enhanced by the fact that it was thrown open to the free purchase of all classes of society, while previous to the reform the higher class alone was entitled to own it. Instead of abandoning the tillage of the fields, according to the expectation of some pessimists, the liberated serf soon became the regular farmer of the lands possessed by the gentry, and entire village communities have been seen during these last few years renting, under conditions of mutual responsibility, the land of a neighbouring estate.

If we investigate the indirect results of the great reform accomplished by the Emperor Alexander, we are first struck by the fact that it involved the necessity of a complete change in provincial administration. Justice and police had hitherto been in the hands of persons elected by the nobility. This could no longer be tolerated the moment the serf was liberated from his previous subjection to the noble and squire. A system of provincial self-government, based on the principle of representation of the whole landowning class, both private proprietors and those possessing land in common, was introduced in its stead. The organisation of justice was completely changed, learned jurists occupying the place of the ignorant magistrates of old who had been appointed by the provincial gentry. The people, as members of juries, were admitted to a share in the exercise of criminal justice. The transformation of the mediæval State into one that answered to the requirements of modern civilisation would have been completed if the Liberator of millions had not been slaughtered on the very day on which he had undertaken to give a constitution to his people.

Years of violent reaction have followed. The feudal party, whose secret designs had been defeated by the mode in which emancipation had been effected, again got the upper hand; and modern Russia now looks back to the period of 1861 as the golden age of Russian Liberalism. It is in the work of the men who were directly engaged in carrying out the great reform that Russian Liberals seek consolation and help; and the Nineteenth of February has become for them a day of general and of grateful commemoration.

# INDEX.

## Reprints of the Legal Classics Published by The Lawbook Exchange, Ltd.

### Admiralty & Maritime Law

**Flanders, Henry. [1824-1911].** *A Treatise on Maritime Law.* Boston: Little, Brown and Company, 1852. xvi, 444 pp. Reprinted 1999 by The Lawbook Exchange, Ltd. ISBN 1-886363-72-2. Cloth. $75.

**Kulsrud, Carl J.** *Maritime Neutrality to 1780. A History of the Main Principles Governing Neutrality and Belligerency to 1780.* Boston: Little, Brown, and Company, 1936. x, 351 pp. LC 99-38825. ISBN 1-58477-027-9. Reprint available March 2000 by The Lawbook Exchange, Ltd. Cloth. New. $65.

**Marsden. R.[eginald]. G.[odfrey], ed.** *Documents Relating to Law and Custom of the Sea.* [n.p.]: The Navy Record Society, 1915-6. Two volumes. xxxiii, 561; xl, 457, [5] pp. Reprinted 1999 by The Lawbook Exchange, Ltd. LCCN 99-24138. ISBN 1-886363-96-X. Cloth. $175.

**[Twiss, Sir Travers].** *The Black Book of the Admiralty, with an Appendix.* Monumenta Juridica. Edited by Sir Travers Twiss. Four volumes. 4, xciii, 491, [2]; 4, lxxxvii, 500, 31; 4, lxxxvi, 673, [1], 31; 4, clii, 559, 32 pp. LCCN 97-38809 ISBN 1-886363-39-0. 1871. Reprinted 1998 by The Lawbook Exchange, Ltd. Cloth. $495.

### Law & Literature

**Barton, Dunbar Plunket.** *Shakespeare and the Law.* With a foreword by James M. Beck. Boston: Houghton Mifflin Company, 1929. xl, 167 pp. Reprint available October 1999 by The Lawbook Exchange, Ltd. LCCN 99-26602. ISBN 1-58477-000-7. Cloth. $60.

**Darrow, Clarence.** *A Persian Pearl. And Other Essays.* East Aurora, NY: The Roycroft Shop, 1899. 175 pp. Reprinted 1997 by The Lawbook Exchange, Ltd. ISBN 1-886363-27-7. Cloth. $50.

**Darrow, Clarence S.** *An Eye for an Eye.* New York: Fox Duffield & Company, 1905. 213 pp. Reprinted 1996 by The Lawbook Exchange, Ltd. ISBN 1-886363-07-2. Cloth. $40.

**Davis, C.K.** *The Law in Shakespeare.* Washington, D.C.: Washington Law Book Co., [1883]. 303 pp. Reprinted 1999 by The Lawbook Exchange, Ltd. ISBN 1-886363-75-7. Cloth. $60.

**Gest, John Marshall.** *The Lawyer in Literature.* London: Sweet & Maxwell, Limited, 1913. xii, 249 pp. Reprint available November 1999 by The Lawbook Exchange, Ltd. LCCN99-18365. ISBN 1-886363-90-0. Cloth. $60.

**Holdsworth, William S.** *Charles Dickens as a Legal Historian.* New Haven: Yale University Press, 1929. 157 pp. Reprinted 1995 by The Lawbook Exchange, Ltd. ISBN 1-886363-06-4. Cloth. $40.

## Legal Biography

**Foss, Edward.** *A Biographical Dictionary of the Judges of England From the Conquest to the Present Time 1066-1870.* London: John Murray, 1870. xv, 792 pp. Reprint available February 2000 by The Lawbook Exchange, Ltd. LCCN 99-12577. ISBN 10886363-86-2. Cloth. $100.

**Richards, John T.** *Abraham Lincoln The Lawyer-Statesman.* Boston: Houghton Mifflin, 1916. Frontis. Illustrated. xii, 260 pp. Reprint available November 1999 by The Lawbook Exchange, Ltd. LCCN 99-20587. ISBN 1-886363-94-3. Cloth. $60.

**Townsend, William H.** *Lincoln the Litigant.* Boston: Houghton Mifflin Company, 1925. [ix], [117] pp. Frontis. Illus. Reprint available February 2000 by The Lawbook Exchange, Ltd. LCCN 99-16499. ISBN 1-58477-021-X. Cloth. $60.

## Legal Codes

**[Field Codes]. [New York 1850-1865]. New York Field Codes. 1850-1865.**
**Vol. I.** *The Code of Civil Procedure of the State of New-York, Reported Complete by the Commissioners on Practice and Pleadings. 1850.*
**Vol. II.** *The Code of Criminal Procedure of the State of New York, Reported Complete by the Commissioners on Practice and Pleadings. 1850.*
**Vol. III.** *The Civil Code of the State of New York, Reported Complete by the Commissioners of the Code. 1865*
**Vol. IV.** *The Penal Code of the State of New York, Reported Complete by the Commissioners of the Code. 1865*
**Vol. V.** *The Political Code of the State of New York. 1860.*
With a new introduction by Michael Weber. Reprinted 1998 by The Lawbook Exchange, Ltd. Five volume series. [8], xcvi, 791; liii, [1], 486; cxii, 776; lxiv, 406, clxvii; xlvii, 607 pp. ISBN 1-886363-40-4 (set). Cloth. $495.

**Livingston, Edward.** *A System of Penal Law, for the State of Louisiana: Consisting of A Code of Crimes and Punishments, A Code of Procedure, A Code of Evidence, A Code of Reform and Prison Discipline, A Book of Definitions. Prepared Under the Authority of a Law of the Said State. To Which are Prefixed a Preliminary Report on the Plan of a Penal Code, and Introductory Reports to the Several Codes Embraced in the System of Penal Law.* Philadelphia: James Kay, Jun. & Brother, 1833.v, 745 pp. Reprint available November 1999 by The Lawbook Exchange, Ltd. LCCN 99-11403. ISBN 1-886363-83-8. Cloth. $95.

## Legal Dictionaries

**Anderson, William C.** *A Dictionary of Law, Consisting of Judicial Definitions and Explanations of Words, Phrases, and Maxims, and an Exposition of the Principles of Law: Comprising a Dictionary and Compendium of American and English Jurisprudence.* Chicago: T.H. Flood and Company, 1889. viii, 1140pp. Reprinted 1996 by The Lawbook Exchange, Ltd. ISBN 1-886363-23-4. Cloth. $125.

**Black, Henry Campbell.** *A Law Dictionary. Containing Definitions of the Terms and Phrases of American and English Jurisprudence, Ancient and Modern. And Including the Principal Terms of International, Constitutional, Ecclesiastical and Commercial Law, and Medical Jurisprudence, with a Collection of Legal Maxims, Numerous Select Titles from the Roman, Modern Civil, Scotch, French, Spanish, and Mexican Law, and Other Foreign Systems, and a Table of Abbreviations.* St. Paul, Minn.: West Publishing, 1910. 1314 pp. Reprinted 1995 by The Lawbook Exchange, Ltd. ISBN 1-886363-10-2. Cloth. $125.

**Black, Henry Campbell.** *A Dictionary of Law. Containing Definitions of the Terms and Phrases of American and English Jurisprudence, Ancient and Modern. Including the Principal Terms of International, Constitutional, and Commercial Law; with a Collection of Legal Maxims and Numerous Select Titles from the Civil Law and Other Foreign Systems.* St. Paul, Minn.. West Publishing, 1891. x, 1253 pp. Reprinted 1991 by The Lawbook Exchange, Ltd. ISBN 0-9630106-0-3. $125.

**Bouvier, John.** *A Law Dictionary Adapted to the Constitution and Laws of the United States of America, and of the Several States of the American Union; with References to the Civil and Other Systems of Foreign Law.* Philadelphia: T. & J.W Johnson, 1839. Two volumes. 559; 28 pp. Reprinted 1993 by The Lawbook Exchange, Ltd. ISBN 0-9630106-7-0. Cloth. $130.

**Burrill, Alexander M.** *A New Law Dictionary and Glossary: Containing Full Definitions of the Principal Terms of the Common and Civil Law, Together with*

*Translations and Explanations of the Various Technical Phrases in Different Languages, Occurring in the Ancient and Modern Reports, and Standard Treatises; Embracing Also All the Principal Common and Civil Law Maxims. Compiled on the Basis of Spelman's Glossary, and Adapted to the Jurisprudence of the United States; with Copious Illustrations, Critical and Historical.* New York: John S. Voorhies, 1850. Two volumes. xviii, 1099 pp. Reprinted 1998 by The Lawbook Exchange, Ltd. LC 97-38481. ISBN 1-886363-32-3. Cloth. $175.

**Holthouse, Henry James.** *A New Law Dictionary, Containing Explanations of Such Technical Terms and Phrases As Defined in the Works of Legal Authors, in the Practice of the Courts, and in the Parliamentary Proceedings of the Houses of Lords and Commons, To Which Is Added An Outline of An Action at Law and of A Suit in Equity. Edited, from the Second and Enlarged London Edition, With Numerous Additions, by Henry Penington.* Philadelphia: Lea and Blanchard, 1847. viii, [17]-495 pp. Reprinted 1999 by The Lawbook Exchange, Ltd. ISBN 1-886363-67-6. Cloth. $75.

**Jacob, Giles. [1686-1744].** *The Law-Dictionary: Explaining the Rise, Progress, and Present State of the English Law; Defining and Interpreting the Terms or Words of Art; and Comprising Copious Information on the Subjects of Law, Trade, and Government. Corrected and Greatly Enlarged by T[homas] E[dlyne] Tomlins.* New York: Printed for, and Published by I. Riley, 1811. Originally six volumes, viii, 531; [2], 543; [2],618; [2], 472; [2], 553; [2], 471pp. Reprint available January 2000 by The Lawbook Exchange, Ltd. ISBN 1-886363-68-4. Cloth. $495.

**Rapalje, Stewart and Lawrence, Robert L.** *A Dictionary of American and English Law with Defintions of the Technical terms of the Canon and Civil Laws. Also, Containing a Full Collection of Latin Maxims, and Citations of Upwards of Forty Thousand Reported Cases, in which Words and Phrases Have Been Judicially Defined or Construed.* Jersey City: Frederick C. Linn & Co., 1888. Two volumes. xxxviii, 1380 pp. Reprinted 1997 by The Lawbook Exchange, Ltd. LC 97-38484. ISBN 1-886363-33-1. Cloth. $195.

**Stimson, Frederic Jesup.** *Glossary of Technical Terms, Phrases, and Maxims of the Common Law.* Boston: Little, Brown, and Company, 1881. iv, 305pp. Reprinted 1999 by The Lawbook Exchange, Ltd. ISBN 1-886363-70-6. Cloth. $60.

**Tayler, Thomas.** *The Law Glossary: Being a Selection of the Greek, Latin, Saxon, French, Norman and Italian Sentences, Phrases, and Maxims, Found in the Leading English and American reports, and Elementary Works.* New York: Lewis & Blood, 1856. 580 pp. Reprinted 1995 by The Lawbook Exchange, Ltd. ISBN 1-886363-12-9. Cloth. $65.

## Legal History

**Bar, Carl Ludwig von.** *A History of Continental Criminal Law.* Boston: Little, Brown, and Company, 1916. lvi, 561 pp. Reprint available October 1999 by The Lawbook Exchange, Ltd. LCCN 99-32341. ISBN 1-58477-013-9. Cloth. $90.

**[Brandeis, Louis D.].** *Brandeis on Zionism. A Collection of Addresses and Statements by Louis D. Brandeis with a Foreword by Mr. Justice Felix Frankfurter.* Washington, D.C.: Zionist Organization of America, [1942]. viii, 156 pp. Reprinted 1999 by The Lawbook Exchange, Ltd. ISBN 1-886363-60-9. Cloth. $65.

**Calhoun, George M.** *The Growth of Criminal Law in Ancient Greece.* Berkeley: University of California Press, 1927. x, 149 pp. LC 99-43192. ISBN 1-58477-037-6. Reprint available December 1999 by The Lawbook Exchange, Ltd. Cloth. New. $50.

**Corwin, Edward.** *The Doctrine of Judicial Review: Its Legal and Historical Basis and Other Essays.* Princeton: Princeton University Press, 1914. ix, 178 pp. Reprint available December 1999 by The Lawbook Exchange, Ltd. LCCN 99-32362. ISBN 1-58477-011-2. Cloth. $60.

**Darrow, Clarence and William J. Bryan.** The *World's Most Famous Court Trial. Tennessee Evolution Case. A Complete Stenographic Report of the Famous Court Test of the Anti-Evolution Act, at Dayton July 10 to 21, 1925, Including Speeches and Arguments of Attorneys.* Cincinnati: National Book Company, [1925]. [4], 339 pp. Reprinted 1997 by The Lawbook Exchange, Ltd. LC 97-38485. ISBN 1-886363-31-5. Cloth. $65.

**Dawson, John P.** *A History of Lay Judges.* Cambridge, Mass.. Harvard University Press, 1960. viii, [2], 310 pp. Reprinted 1999 by The Lawbook Exchange, Ltd. ISBN 1-886363-69-2. Cloth. $75.

**Evans, E.P.** *The Criminal Prosecution and Capital Punishment of Animals.* New York: E.P Dutton, 1906. x, 384pp. Reprinted 1998 by The Lawbook Exchange, Ltd. LC 98-12801. ISBN 1-886363-52-8. Cloth. $65.

**Forsyth, William.** *History of Trial by Jury* [*Second edition*]. Jersey City: Frederick D. Linn, [1875]. x, 388 pp. Reprinted 1994 by The Lawbook Exchange, Ltd. ISBN 0-9630106-8-9. Cloth. $65.

**Forsyth, William.** *The History of Lawyers. Ancient and Modern.* Boston: Estes & Lauriat, 1875. Illustrated. xvii, 404 pp. Reprinted 1996 by the Lawbook Exchange, Ltd. ISBN 1-886363-14-5. Cloth. $60.

**Fortescue, Sir John. [?1394-1476?].** *The Governance of England: Otherwise Called The Difference between an Absolute and a Limited Monarchy. A Revised Text edited with Introduction, Notes, and Appendices by Charles Plummer.* London: Oxford University Press, 1885. xxiii, 387pp. Reprinted 1999 by The Lawbook Exchange, Ltd. ISBN 1-886363-79-X. Cloth. $65.

**Futrell, William H.** *The History of American Customs Jurisprudence.* New York: Published privately, 1941. 314pp. Reprinted 1998 by The Lawbook Exchange, Ltd. LC 98-11342. ISBN 1-886363-51-X. Cloth. $60.

**Greenidge, A.H.J.** *The Legal Procedure of Cicero's Time.* Oxford: The Clarendon Press, 1901. xiii, 599 pp. Reprint available December 1999 by The Lawbook Exchange, Ltd. LCCN 99-26771. ISBN 1-886363-99-4. Cloth. $85.

**Hale, Matthew.** *The History and Analysis of the Common Law of England.* Stafford: J. Nutt, 1713. [x], 264, [28], 176 pp. Reprint available February 2000 by The Lawbook Exchange, Ltd. LCCN 99-33739. ISBN 1-58477-024-4. Cloth. $85.

**Harper, Robert Francis.** *The Code of Hammurabi King of Babylon. About 2250 B.C. Autographed Text transliteration...* Chicago: The University of Chicago Press, 1904. xxviii, 194, ciii (plates) pp. London: John Murray, 1832. xx, 392, lxxvi pp. Illus. LC 99-23953. ISBN 1-58477-003-1. Reprint available December 1999 by The Lawbook Exchange, Ltd. Cloth. New. $75.

**Harris, Virgil M.** *Ancient, Curious, and Famous Wills.* Boston: Little, Brown, and Company, 1911. xiv, 472 pp. Reprinted 1999 by The Lawbook Exchange, Ltd. LCCN 99-20588. ISBN 1-886363-93-5. Cloth. $75.

**Henderson, Gerard Carl.** *The Position of Foreign Corporations in American Constitutional Law. A Contribution to the History and Theory of Juristic Persons in Anglo-American Law.* Cambridge: Harvard University Press, 1918. xix, 199 pp. Reprint available November 1999 by The Lawbook Exchange, Ltd. LCCN 99-18233. ISBN 1-886363-89-7. Cloth. $50.

**Holdsworth, William S.** *Essays in Law and History.* Edited by A.L. Goodhart and H.G. Hanbury. Oxford: At the Clarendon Press, 1946. xv, 302 pp. Reprinted 1995 by The Lawbook Exchange, Ltd. ISBN 1-886363-13-7. Cloth. $50.

**Holdsworth, W.S.** *The Historians of Anglo-American Law.* New York: Columbia University Press, 1928. 175 pp. Reprinted 1994 by The Lawbook Exchange, Ltd. ISBN 0-9630106-9-7. Cloth. $50.

**Johns, C.H.W** *Babylonian and Assyrian Laws, Contracts and Letters.* Edinburgh: T. & T. Clark, 1904. xxii, 424 pp. LC 99-32862. ISBN 1-58477-022-8. Reprint available December 1999 by The Lawbook Exchange, Ltd. Cloth. New. $75.

**Kovalevsky, Maxime.** *Modern Customs and Ancient Laws of Russia. Being the Ilchester Lectures for 1889-90.* London: David Nutt, 1891. x, 260 pp. Reprint available February 2000 by The Lawbook Exchange, Ltd. LCCN 99-16487. ISBN 1-58477-017-1. Cloth. $65.

**Langdell, C.C. [1826-1906].** *A Selection of Cases on the Law of Contracts. with References and Citations. Prepared for Use as a Text-book in Harvard Law School.* Boston: Little, Brown & Co., 1871. xvi, 1022 pp. Reprinted 1999 by The Lawbook Exchange, Ltd. LCCN 99-28293. ISBN 1-58477-001-5. Cloth. $120.

**[MacDonell, Sir John and Edward Manson].** *Great Jurists of the World.* Edited by Sir John MacDonell and Edward Manson. With an Introduction by Van Vechten Veeder. Boston: Little, Brown, and Company, 1914. Illustrated. xxxii, 607 pp. Reprinted 1997 by The Lawbook Exchange, Ltd. ISBN 1-886363-28-5. Cloth. $95.

**Maitland, Frederick W., et.al.** *A General Survey of Events, Sources, Persons & Movements in Continental Legal History. By Various European Authors.* With an introduction by Albert Kocourek. Boston: Little, Brown, 1912. liii, 754pp. Reprinted 1998 by The Lawbook Exchange, Ltd. LC 98-11159. ISBN 1-886363-47-1. Cloth. $110.

**Maitland, Frederic William.** *Roman Canon Law in the Church of England: Six Essays.* London: Methuen & Co., 1898. vii, 184 pp. Reprinted 1998 by The Lawbook Exchange, Ltd. LC 98-22357. ISBN 1-886363-57-9. Cloth. $65.

**Maitland, Frederick W., et.al.** *Select Essays in Anglo-American Legal History. By Maitland, Pollock, Holmes, Beale, Holdsworth and Others.* Boston: Little, Brown, and Company, 1907. Three volumes. 847; 823; 862 pp. Reprinted 1992 by The Lawbook Exchange, Ltd. LCCN 91-77977. ISBN 0-9630106-0-1. Cloth. $195.

**Maitland, Frederick W., Montague, Francis C.,** *A Sketch of English Legal History.* Edited with Notes and Appendices by James F Colby. New York: G.P. Putnam's Sons, 1915. x, 234pp. LCCN 98-11337. ISBN 1-886363-50-1. Reprinted 1998 by The Lawbook Exchange, Ltd. Cloth. $50.

**Merriam, C.E., Jr.** *History of the Theory of Sovereignty Since Rousseau.* New York: Columbia University Press, [1900]. x, [11]-233 pp. Reprinted 1999 by

The Lawbook Exchange, Ltd. LCCN 98-32385. ISBN 1-886363-76-5. Cloth. $65.

**[Nichols, J.].** *A Collection of all the Wills, Now Known to Be Extant, of the Kings and Queens of England, Princes and Princesses of Wales, and every Branch of the Blood Royal, from the Reign of William the Conqueror, to that of Henry the Seventh Exclusive: With Explanatory Notes and a Glossary.* London: J. Nichols, 1780. x, 434 pp. Reprinted 1999 by The Lawbook Exchange, Ltd. LCCN 99-17114. ISBN 1-886363-87-0. Cloth. $75.

**Ogle, Arthur.** *The Canon Law in Mediaeval England. An Examination of William Lyndwood's "Provinciale," in Reply to the Late Professor F.W Maitland.* London: John Murray, 1912. xv, 220 pp. Reprint available February 2000 by The Lawbook Exchange, Ltd. LCCN 99-33827. ISBN 1-58477-026-0. Cloth. $65.

**Pollock, Sir Frederick.** *The Genius of the Common Law.* New York: The Columbia University Press, 1912. vii, 141 pp. Reprint available February 2000 by The Lawbook Exchange, Ltd. LCCN 99-047160. ISBN 1-58477-043-0-1. Cloth. $55.

**Pollock, Frederick and Frederic William Maitland.** *The History of English Law before the Time of Edward I.* Cambridge: Cambridge University Press, 1898. Two volumes. xxxviii, 688; xiv, 691 pp. Reprinted 1996 by The Lawbook Exchange, Ltd. ISBN 1-886363-22-6. Cloth. $165.

**Reeve, Tapping. [1744-1823].** *The Law of Baron and Femme, of Parent and Child, Guardian and Ward, Master and Servant, and of the Powers of the Courts of Chancery; with an Essay on the Terms Heir, Heirs, Heirs of the Body. Third Edition, With Notes and References to English and American Cases by Amasa J. Parker and Charles E. Baldwin, Counselors-At-Law.* Albany: William Gould, 1862. xlvi, 677pp. LCCN 98-36057. ISBN 1-886363-58-7. Reprinted 1998 by The Lawbook Exchange, Ltd. Cloth. $75.

**Pulling, Alexander.** *The Order of the Coif.* London: William Clowes & Sons, Limited, 1884. xii, 288 pp. Frontis. Illus. Reprint available February 2000 by The Lawbook Exchange, Ltd. LCCN 99-37829. ISBN 1-58477-025-2. Cloth. $95.

**Sandys, Sir John Edwin.** *Aristotle's Constitution of Athens. A Revised Text with an Introduction Critical and Explanatory Notes Testimonia and Indices. Second edition, Revised and Enlarged.* London: Macmillan & Co., Limited, 1902. xcii, 331 pp. Frontis. Illus. LC 99-23952. ISBN 1-58477-004-X. Reprint available March 2000 by The Lawbook Exchange, Ltd. Cloth. New. $75.

**Schechter, Frank I.** *The Historical Foundations of the Law Relating to Trade-Marks.* New York: Columbia University Press, 1925. xxviii, 211 pp. LC 99-41673. ISBN 1-58477-035-X. Reprint available December 1999 by The Lawbook Exchange, Ltd. Cloth. New. $60.

**Schwartz, Bernard, editor.** *The Code Napoleon and the Common-Law World. The Sesquicentennial Lectures Delivered at The Law Center of New York University December 13-15, 1954.* New York: New York University Press, 1956. x, 438pp. LCCN 98-34100. ISBN 1-886363-59-5. Reprinted 1998 by The Lawbook Exchange, Ltd. Cloth. $65.

**Schwarz, Philip J.** *Twice Condemned: Slaves and the Criminal Laws of Virginia, 1705-1865* [Baton Rouge: Louisiana State University Press]. [1988]. xvi, 354pp. Reprinted 1998 by The Lawbook Exchange, Ltd. LCCN 98-4424 ISBN 1-886363-54-4. Cloth. $75.

**Tucker, Henry St. George.** *Commentaries on the Laws of Virginia. Comprising the Substance of a Course of Lectures Delivered to the Winchester Law School. With an Introduction by David Cobin and Paul Finkelman.* Richmond: Shepherd and Colin, 1846. Two volumes. 34, 468; 24, 512 pp. Reprinted 1998 by The Lawbook Exchange, Ltd. LCCN 97-10313. ISBN 1-886363-26-9. Cloth. $175.

**Vinogradoff, Sir Paul.** *Outlines of Historical Jurisprudence.* London: Oxford University Press, 1920. Two volumes. 428; x, 315 pp. Reprinted 1999 by The Lawbook Exchange, Ltd. LCCN 98-42298. ISBN 1-886363-64-1. Cloth. $150.

**Walker, James.** *The Theory of the Common Law.* Boston: Little, Brown and Co., 1852. xxiv, 130pp. Reprinted 1998 by The Lawbook Exchange, Ltd. LCCN 98-9522. ISBN 1-886363-45-5. Cloth. $65.

**Warren, Charles.** *History of the Harvard Law School and of Early Legal Conditions in America.* New York: Lewis Publishing Company, 1908. Three volumes. xiv, 543; iv, 560; 397 pp. Illustrated. Reprint available September 1999 by The Lawbook Exchange, Ltd. LCCN 99-29193. ISBN 1-58477-006-6. Cloth. $275.

**Wiener, Leo.** *Commentary to the Germanic Laws and Mediaeval Documents.* Cambridge: Harvard University Press, 1915. lxi, 224 pp. Reprint available October 1999 by The Lawbook Exchange, Ltd. LCCN 99-23969. ISBN 1-58477-005-8. Cloth. $60.

## ☙ Legal Reference and Bibliography ☙

**Benedict, Russell.** *Acts and Laws of the Thirteen Original Colonies and States: Constituting the extraordinary collection of Hon. Russell Benedict.* New York: American Art Association, 1922. [272]pp. Reprinted 1998 The Lawbook Exchange, Ltd. LCCN 98-20196 ISBN 1-886363-56-0. Cloth. $85.

**Eller, Catherine Spicer.** *The William Blackstone Collection in the Yale Law Library. A Bibliographical Catalogue.* New Haven: Yale University Press, 1938. Reprinted 1993 by the Lawbook Exchange, Ltd. xvii, 113 pp. Cloth. LCCN 99-38826. ISBN 0-9630106-5-4. $40.

**Finkelman, Paul**. *Slavery in the Courtroom. An Annotated Bibliography of American Cases.* Washington:Library of Congress, 1985. Illustrated. xxvii, 312pp. Reprinted 1998 by The Lawbook Exchange, Ltd. LCCN 98-11284. ISBN 1-886363-48-X. Cloth. $85.

**Friend, William L.** *Anglo-American Legal Bibliographies. An Annotated Guide.* Washington, D.C.. United States Government Printing Office, 1944. xii, 166 pp. Reprinted 1996 by The Lawbook Exchange, Ltd. ISBN 1-886363-21-8. Cloth. $65.

**Hicks, Frederick.** *Men and Books Famous in the Law. With an introduction by Harlan F Stone.* Rochester, New York: Lawyers Co-operative Publishing, 1921. 259 pp. Reprinted 1992 by The Lawbook Exchange, Ltd. LCCN 92-070809. ISBN 0-9630106-2-X. Cloth.$50.

**Jackson, E. Hilton.** *Latin for Lawyers. Containing I: A Course in Latin, with Legal Maxims and Phrases As a Basis of Instruction. II. A Collection of Over One Thousand Latin Maxims, with English Translations, Explanatory Notes, and Cross-References. III. A Vocabulary of Latin Words.* London: Sweet & Maxwell, 1915. viii, 300 pp. Reprinted 1992 by The Lawbook Exchange, Ltd. LCCN 92-074408. ISBN 0-9630106-4-6. Cloth. $50.

**McNamara, M. Frances.** *Ragbag of Legal Quotations.* Albany: Matthew Bender & Company, 1960. xi, 334 pp. Reprinted 1992 by The Lawbook Exchange, Ltd. LC 92-074141. ISBN 0-9630106-3-8. Cloth. $50.

**Maxwell, W. Harold and C.R. Brown.** *A Complete List of British and Colonial Law Reports and Legal Periodicals. Arranged in Alphabetical and in Chronological Order with Bibliographical Notes.* **[With]:** *Check List of Canadian and Newfoundland Statutes.*[Third Edition]. Toronto: The Carswell Company, Limited, 1937. viii, 141, 49 pp. Reprinted 1995 by The Lawbook Exchange, Ltd. ISBN 1-886363-11-0. Cloth. $70.

**[Worrall, John and Edward Brooke].** *Bibliotheca Legum Angliae. Or, a Catalogue of the Common and Statute Law Books of This Realm, and Some Others Relating Thereto: Giving an Account of Their Several Editions, Ancient Printers, Dates, and Prices, and Wherein They Differ. [With a Supplement to 1800]. Part I Compiled by John Worrall, Part II and Supplement Compiled by Edward Brooke. Parts I, II and Supplement bound in one volume.* London: Printed for Edward Brooke, 1788-1800. 316; 264; 48 pp. 1788-1800. Reprinted 1997 by The Lawbook Exchange, Ltd. ISBN 1-886363-29-3. Cloth. $110.

## ☙ Legal Sources ☙

**Bouvier, John. [1787-1851].** *Institutes of American Law. New Edition by Daniel A. Gleason. In Two Volumes.* Boston:Little, Brown, & Company, 1880. Two volumes. lxviii, 651; iv, 798pp. Reprint available December 1999 by The Lawbook Exchange, Ltd. LCCN 98-54288. ISBN 1-886363-80-3. Cloth. $265.

**[Cardozo, Benjamin].** *Law is Justice. Notable Opinions of Mr. Justice Cardozo.* Foreword by Robert F Wagner. Edited by A.L. Sainer. New York: Ad Press Ltd., [1938]. xvii, 441 pp. Frontis. Reprint available September 1999 by The Lawbook Exchange, Ltd. LCCN 99-34154. ISBN 1-58477-010-4. Cloth. $75.

**[Cherokee Laws].** *Compiled Laws of the Cherokee Nation.* Tahlequah, I.T.:National Advocate Print, 1881. 370pp. LC 98-12741. ISBN 1-886363-42-0. Reprinted 1998 by The Lawbook Exchange, Ltd. With a new introduction by Michael Weber. Cloth. $60.

**Coke, Edward, Sir.** *The First Part of the Institutes of the Laws of England, or, A commentary upon Littleton...* London, J. & W.T. Clarke, 1823. Two volumes. ccxvi,[606]; iv, [772] pp. LC 99-41675. ISBN 1-58477-033-3. Reprint available December 1999 by The Lawbook Exchange, Ltd. Cloth. New. $195.

**Fortescue, John.** *DeLaudibus Legum Angliae. A Treatise in Commendation of the Laws of England.* With Translation by Francis Gregor. Notes by Andrew Amos and a Life of the Author by Thomas (Fortescue) Lord Clermont. Cincinnati: Robert Clarke & Co., 1874. Reprint available September 1999 by The Lawbook Exchange, Ltd. LCCN 99-16485. ISBN 1-58477-019-8. Cloth. $65.

**[St. Germain, Christopher]. [1460-1540].** *The Doctor and Student or Dialogues Between a Doctor of Divinity and a Student in the Laws of England Containing the Grounds of Those Laws Together with Questions and Cases Concerning the Equity*

*Thereof Revised and Corrected by William Muchall, Gent. to which are added two pieces concerning Suits in Chancery by Subpoena.* Cincinnati:Robert Clarke & Co., 1874. xiv, 401pp. Reprinted 1998 by The Lawbook Exchange, Ltd. LCCN 98-11338. ISBN 1-886363-49-8. Cloth. $65.

**Woodbine, George E.** *Four Thirteenth Century Law Tracts. A Thesis Presented to the Faculty of the Graduate Schol of Yale University in Candidacy for the Degree of Doctor of Philosophy.* New Haven: Yale University Press, 1910. vi, 183 pp. Reprint available October 1999 by The Lawbook Exchange, Ltd. LCCN 99-29294. ISBN 1-58477-007-4. Cloth. $50.

## ***Legal Treatises***

**Beck, Theodric Romeyn.** *Elements of Medical Jurisprudence.* Albany: Websters and Skinners, 1823. Two volumes. xxxiv, 418; viii, [9]-471 pp. Reprinted 1997 by The Lawbook Exchange, Ltd. ISBN 1-886363-24-2. Cloth. $125.

**Calabresi, Guido.** *A Common Law for the Age of Statutes.* Cambridge: Harvard University Press, 1982. xi, 319 pp. LC 99-44889. ISBN 1-58477-040-6. Reprint available December 1999 by The Lawbook Exchange, Ltd. Cloth. New. $85.

**Freeman, A.C.** *A Treatise of the Law of Judgments. Including All Final Determinations of the Rights of Parties in Actions or Proceedings at Law or in Equity. Revised, and Greatly Enlarged by Edward W Tuttle.* San Francisco: Bancroft-Whitney, 1925. Three volumes. 1216; 1280; 1264 pp. Reprinted 1993 by The Lawbook Exchange, Ltd. ISBN 0-9630106-6-2. Cloth. $295.

**Gilmore, Grant.** *Security Interests in Personal Property.* Boston: Little, Brown & Company, 1965. Two volumes. xxxiv, 651; xiii, 653-1508 pp. Reprinted 1999 by The Lawbook Exchange, Ltd. LCCN 99-10258. ISBN 1-886363-81-1. Cloth. $195.

**Pomeroy, John N.** *A Treatise on Equity Jurisprudence As Administered in the United States of America. Adapted for All the States and to the Union of Legal and Equitable Remedies under the Reformed Procedure.* San Francisco and New York: Bancroft-Whitney and Lawyers Cooperative, 1941. Five volumes. 914; 1134; 1063; 1104; 716 pp. Reprinted 1995 by The Lawbook Exchange, Ltd. ISBN 1-886363-05-6. Cloth. $450.

**Pothier, Robert Joseph [1699-1772].** *A Treatise on Obligations, Considered in a Moral and Legal View. Translated from the French of Pothier. Translated by Francois-Xavier Martin.* Newburn, N.C.: Martin & Ogden, 1802. Reprint available December 1999 by The Lawbook Exchange, Ltd. With a new introduction by Warren M. Billings. LC 98-38360. ISBN 1-886363-62-5. Cloth. $75.

**Pothier, R.J.** *Treatise on the Contract of Sale.* Translated from the French by L.S. Cushing. Boston: Charles C. Little and James Brown, 1889. xvi, 406 pp. LC 99-10260. ISBN 1-886363-82-X. Reprint available December 1999 by The Lawbook Exchange, Ltd. Cloth. New. $70.

**[Ricardo, David]. McCulloch, J.R.** *The Works of David Ricardo, Esq., M.P. with a Notice of the Life and Writings of the Author.* London: John Murray, 1846. xxxiii, 584 pp. LC 99-39612. ISBN 1-58477-028-7. Reprint available March 2000 by The Lawbook Exchange, Ltd. Cloth. New. $90.

**Sears, John H.** *Trust Estates as Business Companies. [Second Edition].* Kansas City, Mo.:Vernon Law Book Company, 1921. xx, 782 pp. [1921]. Reprinted June 1998 by The Lawbook Exchange, Ltd. LCCN 97-32423 ISBN 1-886363-41-2. Cloth. $95.

## ☙ Philosophy of Law ☙

**Austin, John.** *The Province of Jurisprudence Determined.* London: John Murray, 1832. xx, 392, lxxvi pp. LC 99-33457. ISBN 1-58477-023-6. Reprint available December 1999 by The Lawbook Exchange, Ltd. Cloth. New. $75.

**Fuller, Lon L.** *The Law in Quest of Itself.* Boston: Beacon Press, 1966. [vi], 150 pp. Reprint available October 1999 by The Lawbook Exchange, Ltd. LCCN 99-32863. ISBN 1-58477-016-3. Cloth. $45.

**Jhering, Rudolf Von.** *Law as a Means to an End.* Translated from the German by Isaac Husik with an Editorial Preface by Joseph H. Drake and with Introductions by Henry Lamm and W.M. Geldart. Boston: The Boston Book Company, 1913. lxi, 483 pp. Reprinted 1999 by The Lawbook Exchange, Ltd. LCCN 99-23754. ISBN 1-58477-009-0. Cloth. $80.

**Jhering, Rudolph von.** *The Struggle for Law. Translated from the Fifth German Edition by John J. Lalor. Second Edition, with an Introduction by Albert Kocourek.* Chicago: Callaghan and Company, 1915. lii, 138 pp. Reprinted 1997 by The Lawbook Exchange, Ltd. ISBN 1-886363-25-0. Cloth. $60.

**Kelsen, Hans. [1881-1973].** *General Theory of Law and State.* Translated by Anders Wedberg. Cambridge: Harvard University Press, 1945. xxxiii, 516pp.

LCCN 98-32334. ISBN 1-886363-74-9. Reprinted 1999 by The Lawbook Exchange, Ltd. Cloth. $75.

**Pollock, Sir Frederick.** *The Genius of the Common Law.* New York: The Columbia University Press, 1912. vii, 141 pp. Reprint available February 2000 by The Lawbook Exchange, Ltd. LCCN 99-047160. ISBN 1-58477-043-0-1. Cloth. $55.

**Radin, Max.** *Law as Logic and Experience.* New Haven: Yale University Press, 1940. ix, [1], 171 pp. Reprint available February 2000 by The Lawbook Exchange, Ltd. LCCN 99-30670. ISBN 1-58477-008-2. Cloth. $55.

**Vinogradoff, Paul.** *Custom and Right.* Oslo: H. Aschehoug, 1925. 110 pp. LC 99-0474851. ISBN 1-58477-048-1. Reprint available March 2000 by The Lawbook Exchange, Ltd. Cloth. New. $45.

## Special Editions

**Stokes, I.N. Phelps.** *The Iconography of Manhattan Island 1498-1909* New York: Robert H. Dodd, 1915. Six volumes. Reprinted 1998 by The Lawbook Exchange, Ltd. LCCN 97-30604. ISBN 1-886363-30-7. Cloth. $750.

## U.S. Constitutional History

**Bauer, Elizabeth Kelley.** *Commentaries on the Constitution 1790-1860.* New York: Columbia University Press, 1952. 400 pp. Reprinted 1999 by The Lawbook Exchange, Ltd. LCCN 98-45409. ISBN 1-886363-66-8. Cloth. $75.

**Beard, Charles A.** *The Supreme Court and the Constitution.* New York: The Macmillan Company, 1912. vii, 127 pp. Reprinted 1999 by The Lawbook Exchange, Ltd. LCCN 98-50368. ISBN 1-886363-78-1. Cloth. $45.

**Bondy, William.** *Separation of Governmental Powers in History, in Theory, and in the Constitutions.* New York: Columbia College, 1896. Reprinted 1999 by The Lawbook Exchange, Ltd. vi,[7]-185, [1] pp. LCCN 98-44994. ISBN 1-886363-65-X. Cloth. $65.

**Cohn, Morris M.** *An Introduction to the Study of the Constitution; A Study showing the play of Physical and Social Factors in the Creation of Institutional Law.* Baltimore: The Johns Hopkins Press, 1892. xi, 235 pp. LC 99-38730. ISBN

1-58477-032-5. Reprint available March 2000 by The Lawbook Exchange, Ltd. Cloth. New. $50.

**Cooley, Thomas McIntyre.** *A Treatise on the Constitutional Limitations Which Rest Upon the Legislative Power of the States of the American Union. [1st edition]*. Boston: Little, Brown, and Co., 1868. xlvii, 720pp. Reprinted 1999 by The Lawbook Exchange, Ltd. LCCN 99-20589. ISBN 1-886363-92-7. Cloth. $95.

**Cooley, Thomas M.** *A Treatise on the Constitutional Limitations which Rest Upon the Legislative Power of the States of the American Union. Fifth edition.* Boston: Little, Brown, and Co., 1883. lxxxi, 886pp. Reprinted October 1998 by The Lawbook Exchange, Ltd. LCCN 98-12730. ISBN 1-886363-53-6. Cloth. $120.

**Dodd, Walter Fairleigh.** *The Revision and Amendment of State Constitutions.* Baltimore: The Johns Hopkins Press, 1910. xvii, 350 pp. Reprinted 1999 by The Lawbook Exchange, Ltd. ISBN 1-886363-73-0. Cloth. $65.

**Duer, William Alexander.** *A Course of Lectures on the Constitutional Jurisprudence of the United States; Delivered Annually in Columbia College, New York. The Second Edition, Revised, Enlarged, and Adapted to Professional as well as General Use.* Boston: Little, Brown & Co., 1856. xxiv, 545 pp. LC 99-16385. ISBN 1-58477-020-1. Reprint available December 1999 by The Lawbook Exchange, Ltd. Cloth. New. $85.

**Fisher, Sydney George.** *The Evolution of the Constitution of the United States. Showing That It Is a Development of Progressive History and Not an Isolated Document Struck Off at a Given Time or an Imitation of English or Dutch Forms of Government.* Philadelphia: J.B. Lippincott, 1897. 398 pp. Reprinted 1996 by The Lawbook Exchange, Ltd. LCCN 97-41054. ISBN 1-886363-08-0. Cloth. $65.

**Flanders, Henry.** *An Exposition of the Constitution of the United States. Designed as a Manual of Instruction.* Philadelphia: E.H. Butler & Co., 1860. xii, 311 pp. Reprint available October 1999 by The Lawbook Exchange, Ltd. LCCN 99-31594. ISBN 1-58477-014-7. Cloth. $60.

**Ford, Paul Leicester.** *Pamphlets on the Constitution of the United States, Published During Its Discussion by the People 1787-1788.* Brooklyn, N.Y., 1888. viii, 451 pp. LC 99-25089. ISBN 1-886363-95-1. Reprint available March 2000 by The Lawbook Exchange, Ltd. Cloth. New. $75.

**Holt, W. Stull.** *Treaties Defeated by the Senate. A Study of the Struggle Between President and Senate Over the Conduct of Foreign Relations.* Baltimore: The Johns Hopkins Press, 1933. vi, [1],328 pp. Reprint available February 2000 by The

Lawbook Exchange, Ltd. LCCN 99-39606. ISBN 1-58477-029-5. Cloth. $65.

**[Madison, James]. Hunt, Gaillard, Scott, James Brown.** *The Debates in The Federal Convention of 1787 Which Framed the Constitution of the United States of America.* New York: Oxford University Press, 1920. xcvii, [1], 731 pp. Reprinted 1999 by The Lawbook Exchange, Ltd. LCCN 98-51911. ISBN 1-886363-77-3. Cloth. $110.

**Minor, Raleigh C.** *Notes on the Science of Government and the Relations of the States to the United States.* [Charlottesville]: University of Virginia, 1913. x, 171 pp. Reprinted 1995 by The Lawbook Exchange,Ltd. ISBN 1-886363-09-9. Cloth. $40.

**Story, Joseph. [1779-1845].** *A Familiar Exposition of the Constitution of the United States: Containing a Brief Commentary on Every Clause, Explaining the True Nature, reasons, and Objects Thereof; Designed for the Use of School, Libraries and General Readers. With an Appendix, Containing Important Public Documents, Illustrative of the Constitution.* New York: Harper & Brothers: 1865. 372 pp. Reprinted 1999 by The Lawbook Exchange, Ltd. ISBN 1-886363-71-4. Cloth. $60.

**[Taylor, John]. [1753-1824].** *A Defence of the Measures of the Administration of Thomas Jefferson. By Curtius.* Washington: Samuel H. Smith, 1804. 136 pp. Reprinted 1999 by The Lawbook Exchange, Ltd. LCCN 99-24139. ISBN 1-886363-97-8. Cloth. $60.

**Taylor, John.** *Construction Construed and Constitutions Vindicated.* Richmond:printed by Shepherd & Pollard, 1820. iv, 344pp. Reprinted 1998 by The Lawbook Exchange, Ltd. LCCN 97-49411. ISBN 1-886363-43-9. Cloth. $65.

**Taylor, John.** *An Inquiry into the Principles and Policy of the Government of the United States.* Fredericksburg:Green and Cady, 1814. With an introduction by Roy Franklin Nichols, Yale University Press, 1950. 562pp. Reprinted 1998 by The Lawbook Exchange, Ltd. LCCN 98-11147. ISBN 1-886363-46-3. Cloth. $75.

**Tucker, Henry St. George.** *Limitations on the Treaty-Making Power Under the Constitution of the United States.* Boston: Little, Brown, and Company, 1915. xxi, 444 pp. Reprint available February 2000 by The Lawbook Exchange, Ltd. LCCN 99-31589. ISBN 1-58477-015-5. Cloth. $75.

**Tucker, St. George.** *Blackstone's Commentaries. With Notes of Reference to the Constitution and Laws, of the Federal Government of the United States, and of the Commonwealth of Virginia. In Five Volumes, with an Appendix to Each volume,*

*Containing Short Tracts upon Such Subjects As Appeared Necessary to Form a Connected View of the Laws of Virginia As a Member of the Federal Union.* Philadelphia: William Young Birch and Abraham Small, 1803. Five volumes. Reprinted 1996 by The Lawbook Exchange, Ltd. ISBN 1-886363-15-3. Cloth. $450.

**[Upshur, Abel Parker].** *A Brief Enquiry Into the True Nature and Character of Our Federal Government, being a review of Judge Story's Commentaries on the Constitution of the United States. By a Virginian.* Petersburg: Printed by Edmund and Julian C. Ruffin, 1840. 132pp. Reprinted 1998 by The Lawbook Exchange, Ltd. LCCN 97-11151. ISBN 1-886363-44-7. Cloth. $45.

**Wright, John S.** *Citizenship Sovereignty.* Chicago: Published for American Citizens, the True Maintainers of State Sovereignty, 1864. Reprinted 1998 by The Lawbook Exchange, Ltd. LCCN 98-15940 ISBN 1-886363-55-2. Cloth. $65.